VETERAN

MINDSET

2.0

SHAWN LAURIE

Copyright © 2021 by Shawn Laurie

All rights reserved. No part of this publication may be reproduced, distributed, or transmitted in any form or by any means, including photocopying, recording, or other electronic or mechanical methods, without the prior written permission of the publisher, except in the case of brief quotations embodied in critical reviews and certain other noncommercial uses permitted by copyright law.

Author assumes all rights, responsibilities, and liability for all content. All stories have been reprinted with permission rights.

Printed by Vet Life 4 Life, United States of America. First printing, April 2021. **ISBN:** 9798737121877

For permission requests, Send to: Attention: Permissions Request Shawn Laurie
739 Harriet Dr
Florence, SC 29501
www.VetLife4Life.com

Front cover image by Jay Perez with 2Ps Studios
https://www.2psstudios.com/

Author Coaching, Book Design, and Publishing by Sean Douglas, Founder of www.TheSuccessCorps.com

Back Cover Headshot Photography by KaceKlicks Photography of Florence
https://www.Facebook.com/kaceklicksphotography

Dedication

First, I want to dedicate this book to my best friend and a fellow Veteran, Delbis Barreiro, my brother who lost his life in 2016 to PTSD/Depression. He has been a huge reason that I decided to dedicate my life to helping those that are struggling after Military Service. He also inspired me to continue my mission by creating a Veteran Non-Profit Organization to help stop the suicide epidemic of 22+ Veterans a day. Next, I want to dedicate this book to my kids. I want them to see that anything is possible if you put your mind to it and work hard. A huge thank you to my wife, Tonya, who has always stood by my side and never gave up on me throughout my Military career. She stuck it out through the deployments, the struggles with addiction, and my mental health conditions. Also, thank you to all the friends that I have made through this journey on social media and in person, especially those who never stopped believing in my ability to write this book and get it finished.

Thank you to my Veteran brothers and sisters that have stood beside me, supported me, and believed in me from the very beginning. I have always said, "I have the best friends and supporters that any person could ever ask for." Also, this book goes to all the Veterans that are currently now, or have ever, struggled with Mental Health & Addiction. It has been my purpose since 2017 to change as many lives as I can. My mission has been and always will be to show others that, "your diagnosis does not define who you are," and to show people that changing the way we think and changing our mindset can change our entire life. I am grateful for the continued support.

TABLE OF CONTENTS

Introduction	i
Chapter 1: Mindset	2
Chapter 2: Acceptance	14
Chapter 3: Focus	25
Chapter 4: Self-Worth	37
Chapter 5: Recovery	45
Conclusion	55
The Practicals Section	59
Mindset	60
Acceptance	66
Focus	72
Self-Worth	81
Recovery	89
Questions	99
Affirmations	116

Introduction

Welcome to Veteran Mindset 2.0. I am excited that you have decided to start focusing on your mindset and have trusted me to help you build a better version of yourself. In this workbook you are going to be introduced to a lot of knowledge that I have learned through my own personal experience with mental health and Addiction. I will be discussing how it affects us all in many of different ways. You will learn many coping skills, techniques and strategies on how to build up your unhealthy mindset and take your life to the 2.0 version and take back control of your life. My purpose for this workbook is not only to take you to a 2.0 Mindset but to teach you everything that I have learned these past 10 years of my experiences struggling with Mental Health and Addiction. I once was that veteran ready to end my own life and give up on everything to the person I am today. A successful speaker, author, Social Media Influencer and a Life Coach and all this in just 3 years. So yes, I am confident this workbook will change your life. The one thing that all of us veterans have in common is the challenges we face trying to adjust back into civilian life. We are all different and we have had different experiences, some of us have been through combat tours and experienced traumatic events. While some other veterans might be struggling with mental health issues like PTSD, Depression, Anxiety, and Anger from outside the military. Maybe a traumatic event happened during your service or maybe not. Maybe you have experienced PTSD, Anxiety or even Depression since childhood or maybe your struggles are an unhealthy Mindset for whatever the reason and now you are looking for a change. I promise that you have come to the right place. I feel like it is my responsibility to make it clear when talking about Veterans with Mental Health that we all understand veterans do not only suffer with Mental Health and Addiction because of combat. Millions of people suffer daily in the U.S and every situation is different. The fact is we are losing 22 plus veterans every day to suicide. My goal is to start putting a huge dent in that number by giving veterans the tools to success and create a 2.0 mindset so you can live a happier and healthier lifestyle. I have been doing research for many years trying to understand why so many of us veterans have the mentality that "We Don't Matter" anymore once we are out of the military. In this workbook I will discuss key points in your life that have been affected by an unhealthy mindset. One of the many purposes of this workbook is to help you understand that your Mental Health does not define who you are. I believe that if you want to take your Mindset to a 2.0 Version, you must address all the negative aspects of your life. Veteran Mindset 2.0 will help you focus on the areas of your life that have been tearing you down. And together we can start rebuilding your Mindset and your new life. VM2.0 will take your Mindset to a place you never thought was possible. You will start living the life you deserve and reaching the goals you have set for yourself. VM2.0 will show you how to turn your negatives into positives and teach you how to use your mindset to turn your whole life around. It will take hard work and make you face many challenges about yourself, but if you keep an open mind and really take the time that is needed to implement everything that I learned from my personal experiences, to all my intensive research in this workbook, you will make some amazing and positive changes in your own life. So, the real question now is this, are you ready to change your life? Are you ready to take your mindset to the 2.0 version and start winning at everything you do? If you want it, you can have it all by reading and taking this workbook seriously. I believe in you, now it is time for you to start believing in yourself. I put a lot of great information together and it is all waiting for you by simply starting with the first chapter. I have put together five key topics in the practicals section of this book you will need to work on to get you to the 2.0 level. I will guide and teach you through my knowledge and experiences that has gotten me where I am today. I am so confident in this that I created these topics in a certain order to help you get to the Veteran Mindset 2.0. In addition to the five topics, I have also broken down each topic into five more in depth "Key Points" that will help you understand each topic better once you read the 5 chapters in this book portion.

Once you finish reading the book chapters and you finish the practicals sections, you will have 80 Questions to answers. I recommend answering the questions after you are finished with all of the reading materials. This will help you understand what it is you need to do and what you have learned. It will also show you the things you need to work on and how to stay in the 2.0 Mindset. Read and understand as much as you can in the chapter book portion and then start the practicals for in depth information on how to get to the Veteran Mindset 2.0.

Here are the 5 topics you will have to learn and understand to get to the next level of your life and mindset:

- ➢ Mindset
- ➢ Acceptance
- ➢ Focus
- ➢ Self-Worth
- ➢ Recovery

Each one of the topics have been carefully written in a way for you to understand it. I have broken down each of these topics and it will guide you to success. You can change your life by changing the way you think and feel about yourself. I will guide you every step of the way. Soon you will be living the best version of yourself and you will become something you never thought possible. You will be living a Veteran Mindset 2.0. Here is my own quote that I live my life by:

"Don't just talk about it, be about it" -Shawn Laurie

CHAPTER 1
Mindset

Changing your mindset is not as easy as some people make it out to be. It takes a lot of work and a lot of practice. I have learned this through many years of my own experience, challenges, and failures. The first thing you will need to understand about upgrading your mindset into a 2.0 version is you need to first realize you have an unhealthy mindset. You must recognize when there are problems and you must want and find the solution. You need to have the desire to make the changes you want. Now, let us talk about Veterans for a moment since most of you reading this probably are one. Veterans have a unique situation. Reason I say that is because we have been broken down from the very beginning and built back up through basic training. Those of us that have been through multiple deployments and many years of service have created a strong mindset. I have also learned that it does not matter how strong we are when we are faced with Traumatic Events, Mental Health, or even Addiction. All these things can cause us to develop an unhealthy mindset and fall into a deep depression, which is one of the many reasons we lose 22 Veterans every day to suicide. We will discuss it more in depth in the "Practicals" section of this workbook. I have been doing research for many years and talking with thousands of Veterans trying to understand this epidemic. I lost my best friend in 2016 to suicide, and in 2017 I almost lost my own battle with Mental Health and Addiction. One of the most common struggles that us Veterans face is transitioning out of the Military into civilian life. It is a huge challenge, especially for those Veterans that have been forced out of the Military because of injuries or something else. A lot of times, we try to get back into the same environment that we left many years ago, but it just does not work. It just does not feel the same anymore. We have a hard time trying to adjust to civilian life. If you spent many years in the Military or any time on combat tours, you understand transitioning is hard. Many of us Veterans just want to get back into the rhythm of things and unfortunately many Veterans never find it. Some of the reasons that I found from my own experiences is that we feel like we do not have the same structures that the Military provided. For example, we are looking for leadership, camaraderie, and direction from our higher ups and it is just not there anymore. When your fresh out of the Military and struggling with your mental health, you just cannot see past the bullshit going on in our head. We want people to understand us, but it seems like nobody does. We want our families and friends to get it, but they just do not understand. We get tired of people thinking we are crazy because of the things we have been through or why we act or say things that do not make sense to them. So, for just for those reasons most of us do not ever talk about what we went through or what we feel, we just hold it all inside causing us to develop a serious unhealthy mindset, or other problems, like substance and alcohol abuse. When you develop an unhealthy mindset, it will start destroying many areas of your life. I have seen it destroy marriages, friendships, careers, and families. It happens all the time. The best thing that ever happened to me is when I finally understood that changing my mindset was all up to me. I had to start focusing on the good things in my life. I had to start focusing on all the great things around me and stop focusing so much on the negativity.

It is not an easy task and takes many techniques and strategies that we will go over in the practicals section. You must understand that you cannot change the things that you have been through. You must accept them for what they are, do what it takes to create a new life, and a new way of thinking. You control your own thoughts, nobody else does. Many of the successful people and business Entrepreneurs will tell you it all starts with your mindset. You must believe in yourself and believe that you can make the changes needed to grow. Once you start making those changes, you will start seeing the results immediately, including in the people around you. All of us just want to live a happy, healthy, and successful life. Another example of why so many of us struggle with our mindset is because of traumatic events that have occurred in or outside the Military. It is common for Veterans to get unsettled and not know how to handle their current situation. They get stressed out and lose focus no longer having a purpose or passion to even the small tasks. Many are prescribed medications and counseling just to feel normal again. It is a terrible feeling we when live on medications just to live a normal life, many times making us feel worse. That is why I have searched for many years for different techniques to help with my mental health and my mindset. There are many ways to take yourself from an unhealthy mindset to a healthy mindset. You will learn many ways that have worked for me and other Veterans. There are no secrets or shortcuts to a happy life. We cannot control the bad things that happen to us, but we can control how we react to them. We choose how we want to think about things. It is up to us to make good things happen. You must continue to fight the good fight, continue to push forward and do your best to become the best version of yourself. "Negative thought's bring negative situations." Focus on the good in your life. Try focusing on the things you enjoy and love. You cannot upgrade your mindset if you are constantly thinking about how shitty your life is. You cannot change anything that is going wrong if you do not accept your reality and work on change.

If you want to change your life, you have to keep pushing forward and doing the things it takes to become more positive and more motivational. Something else that I have learned is people you associate yourself with play a huge part in the kind of mindset you have. Toxic people equal a toxic life and mindset. You must switch it up, start surrounding yourself with people that are not toxic, and find the motivated, inspirational people. Create your own positive environment. You must stick around those people that have the same inspirations and the same intentions as you do. The truth is, most of us have more toxic family members then we do friends. It does not only matter how toxic they are, it is the point you get no support from them either. Having support from people you care about is important for many reasons, especially struggling with depression. Depression can make it easy to get you distracted from your goals and mission. Like I always say, "You cannot control other people. All you can do is do your best to be there for them, and maybe one day things will get better." Keep pushing forward and keep a positive attitude. Keep doing what it takes to reach your goals. Remember, anybody can be successful if they want to be.

You must believe in yourself and know you can do it. Never limit yourself to the easy tasks. If it's hard, that means it will be worth it in the end. Never judge something by how difficult it is. Remember, if it was easy, then everybody would do it. Here is something I talk about often and it is something that millions of people struggle with daily; it is called "Regret." Regret is something that you have done or have not done and now you regret your decisions. That is why it is so important to focus on the now. We cannot change the past, but we can change the future. Regret can stop you from doing great things in the future as well and it can hold you down and make you feel terrible. Not only have I been through it, but I have watched family and friends struggle with things they wish they would have done differently. Trust me, if you have not had regret in your life, I hope for your sake it stays that way. You never want to look back at your life and wished you would have done the things you wanted or needed to do.

You want to keep pushing forward and striving for greatness. You have made mistakes and that is okay. Never stop. Never quit. Believe in yourself and know your self-worth. Accept your situation but look for positive solutions. You can do anything you put your mind to. One of the proudest moments of my life was the day I decided to straighten my life out and get off the drugs and alcohol. I made my mind up and I found a way to get clean and sober. I did what was needed to accomplish my mission and I got it done with determination and will power. I faced my challenge. It gave me more confidence to keep fighting my other issues. The thing about struggling with Mental Health and Addiction is that you must work on one thing at a time. I was still struggling with my PTSD, Depression and Anxiety, but I was no longer on the drugs that was making my conditions worse. I was finally headed in the right direction trying to get to where I am today. Whatever you want to do with your life or the goals you want to reach is completely up to you. Only you can make them happen. Good people in your life can encourage you and help motivate you but you must make the decision and get it done.

You can never lose sight of the things you want to achieve, no matter what age you are. Of course, that clock keeps ticking and you continue to grow older. There will be certain things you may not physically be able to do anymore, but if you believe you can make it happen, then it will. We are all unique and special in our own way. Being a good person is something we choose to be. We can all choose to be evil and full of hate. We can live our life full of regret and anger. It's completely up to us. Anger is a common symptom of PTSD that a lot of Veterans do not realize. It took me many of years to finally understand why I was so angry all the time. Anger is a lot like depression, it can consume you and it will destroy you mentally and emotionally. Anger is one of those things that will tear you down, chew you up, and spit you out if you allow it. It is easy to stay mad and blame the world for your situations. I call that the "victim mentality", blaming everybody for the things that go wrong and what has happened to you, blaming everybody and everything for your problems. Blaming the war, blaming the Military, and blaming the VA is the most common.

Do not get me wrong, if you are a Combat Veteran, have experienced traumatic events and develop PTSD or any other mental health conditions, I agree the Military is responsible but you cannot continue to play the "blame game" your whole life. Now is the time you need to accept what happened and look for solutions and focus on getting better. Hints: (The reason you are reading this workbook and changing your life and mindset) You must get to the point where you take responsibility for your actions and the way you live. A lot of people are put in situations that may be harder than others, but I have also known many of the people that have fought their way out of bad situations. I believe you can use your mindset to manifest a great life. This is how I have changed everything in my life in just three years. Your environment plays a huge role on how you feel. If you are surrounded by anger and sadness every day, you will begin to believe that all that hate, anger, and depression you feel is normal. Change your environment and start looking for role models and mentors to look up to. Find those people that inspire you to do great things and be happy.

Changing your mindset in a good way or a bad way is up to you. Nobody can choose your thoughts for you. There are good and bad people all around us, and like I have been saying, these people can help influence you. Either way, it is still your choice and your decision on how you want to live your life. If you want a 2.0 Mindset, you must work your ass off. Stay on it and keep pushing forward, keep striving for greatness, keep doing the things that it takes to become successful. Nobody is going to do it for you. One thing that I have learned, is if there is something that I need or want, I must work for it and get it myself. There is no such thing as a "Golden Ticket" for Veterans, or anybody for that matter. Generally speaking, you do not get something for nothing. If you do not go to the gym, you will not gain muscles or lose weight. Working toward improving your mental health, addiction, or finances will not only give you what you want or need, but it is a great way to build your self-confidence and self-esteem which ultimately helps you start building up your own self-worth. Anything that you want in your life you will have to work for it. Remember, a victim mindset does not help you. Pats on the back do not pay your bills or feed your kids. Being a victim of a traumatic event, crimes or accidents, do happen daily. I myself have had many events that I still struggle with, but if I had the victim mindset, that would make my life much worse.

The point is that living that type of mindset will keep you down and stop you from becoming successful, because you are not focusing on the solution. I have met and talked with thousands of Veterans that have lost everything, including their arms and legs, and sometimes, both. I have seen Veterans that have lost loved ones during deployments, car wrecks, struggling with family members dying, and family members burying their own children from suicide. There is no doubt that there is a lot of pain out here in this world, but it is how you handle those situations that will make a difference in your life. 22 Veterans that we lose every day to suicide is real. Traumatic events and struggles happen every day, but it is up to you to make the best out of every situation. It is ok to feel sad, angry, and upset, and so on because those are all human emotions. You cannot run away from being human. There does come a time when you have to face reality and say, "You know what, I'm tired of living this way", and when that time comes, you must do what you need to do just like when we were in the Military. They gave us the tools we needed to grow. We were taught Leadership, Accountability, and Decision-Making skills. They gave us the mission and we would execute it. The idea was to take all these skills we learned in the Military and apply it to civilian life, but as we have seen it does not always work out that way. This workbook is the same way in many ways. The things you have learned here is not an overnight process. You will not read this workbook and have a Veteran 2.0 Mindset the next day. You must practice what you have learned every day which takes hard work, dedication, and willpower. Always remind yourself you only have one life to live. Let us all make it the best life we can possibly have! Always love your family, love your kids, love your friends, and show love and compassion to strangers, but always defend yourself when you feel like you need to.

By you living this way, those same type of people will be drawn to you. Be a strong person and always lead by example. Teach others how to also be Leaders. If you want more Leaders and success in your life, you must step up and show people how. Not only are you changing your own life, but you are changing the lives around you and that is an amazing feeling. This is one reason why I got into Personal Development and helping others, because it just gives me such a great feeling to know that my experiences and my knowledge can help other people that are struggling. Once you develop the 2.0 Mindset, you will feel like you have no choice but to help others that struggle because you feel like it is your responsibility. It's what most successful people have a passion to do, but remember, before you get to that place of helping others with their problems, you must start by focusing and addressing yourself first. You cannot help others when your life is in troubled waters.

Always remember you cannot force others to change. They must be ready for change on their own time just like you and I had to do. In the beginning, I learned this the hard way, but as I started growing and changing my mindset, I eventually realized that no matter how many videos, Facebook lives, support groups, phone calls, or events I spoke at, I cannot force people to change. I cannot make anybody do what they don't want to do. People change because they are ready to change. So, the most important thing you can do right now is to focus on yourself and get your own mindset right, because this is your life and you make your own decisions.

One day you will look back and you will be proud of yourself for making the right choices and positive changes. We are given choices in this life and it is up to all of us to make the right choices. Even through the hard times, we have the choice to either give up or keep pushing through. Something that a lot of people don't realize is that when you push through the tough times, that is when you will see the rewards. Remember the old saying "No Pain, No Gain"? I never knew how true that was until I woke up and seen it for myself. Unfortunately, most people with an unhealthy mindset will give up when times get hard.

If you learn to control the negative thoughts and not allowing them to consume you, you can change your negativity into positivity by reminding yourself of the rewards you'll receive for getting through those hard days. In other words, life might be hard, but if you stick with it, you will gain success in the end. Remember, success is more than just money, it's about happiness and living your life with purpose and passion. Let's talk about having success with this workbook and what your goals are. It may take you three months, or 12 months, or even longer. If you stick with it and push yourself to your limits, you will change your mindset to a 2.0 version which includes a positive change to your whole life. You will become a more positive, happier person. Your life will start to change in so many positive ways that you will forget what it's like to be unhappy.

It can take a long time to be successful mentally and financially. It takes a lot of practice to upgrade your mindset and build a positive lifestyle. If you believe you can do it, it is going to happen. How soon you reach success depends on how soon you get started. Deciding your worth is all up to you, nobody else can decide your self-worth for you. If you feel like you are literally not worth anything, then that's how others might start looking at you. If you have low self-esteem, a lot of people can see it and feel the low energy you share. Most will look at you the same way that you look at yourself. That is, we celebrate winners, because they look like it and feel like it and it makes us all want to win. However, nobody's negative opinion about you matters. You must learn to overlook those that hate you or dislike you. It is a whole different feeling when people love and care about you. If we see you for who you really are as a good person, that builds up your confidence about yourself.

CHAPTER

2

Acceptance

Accepting your current situation is absolutely another key factor to get to the next level in your life. What's most important to understand is that Acceptance is the second step of the process in the journey to a 2.0 Mindset. There are many ways that I will teach and encourage you about Acceptance in this workbook. We will go over it more in depth once you begin the practicals section on Acceptance. Right now, in this chapter, I will explain briefly on some other important steps, discuss what you need to do for you to learn and understand how to accept your situation, and why it is important to understand what Acceptance means to get to the next level. Once you have made the decision that you are ready to upgrade your mindset and make the changes needed in your life, you are now ready to accept the situation you are in. You must accept everything that has happened to you in the past, as well as, what is happening in the present. The first step to Acceptance is knowing the difference between "knowing it" and "accepting it." You already know all the struggles that you have been through in the past, but knowing and admitting those struggles is only half the challenge.

The other half is you must accept all those struggles that you have been through and what you are currently going through. You must now face them, focus on the solutions, and learn how to move forward in a positive direction. You will soon understand the difference between knowing and accepting your situation, because you can know something about yourself without accepting it. In other words, you are in denial and you need to get yourself out of that mindset. You must stop lying and telling yourself you are not struggling. Trust me, I know that most of us would rather just keep moving forward and not even think about any issues that we have, and to keep our problems hidden away as to not bother people with them. I get it, I promise. There are so many reasons for accepting your problems and you will understand so much more once you start making progress.

Let's discuss why we hide our feelings in the first place and why we feel the need to suppress our emotions. One of the main reasons why we do this is because of what I have seen and heard from others that have dealt with these things, including with my own experiences. There is this thing called a "stigma" I am sure you have heard of. Another word commonly used is "stereotype." When I first started researching and understanding how serious this stigma was with Mental Health, it came from some of my Vietnam Veteran brothers who have been struggling with Mental Health and addictions for over 40 years. Here is just one

ACCEPTANCE

example of the stigma that surrounds Vietnam Veterans. I am sure you have probably seen the TV shows and the movies that only show Vietnam Veterans that are all crazy drunks, are violent, addicts and pot heads. Just another stereotype that the world is shown. This is so untrue and unfair to label all of them like that. Yes, many do struggle with mental health issues and addiction, but the example shows how all of them are labeled that way. This stigma is not just in the Military or even just in our Veteran communities. It has been infiltrated in our society today in Schools, Colleges, LEOs, EMS, Fire, and many other Agencies and Companies.

I have talked with many people that tried talking with their higher ups about personal issues like Mental Health or even addiction, and all of them have been fired, demoted, and placed on administration leave just for being honest. I was personally fired from Walmart because I told my manager I was struggling with addiction and my car was repossessed and I needed help, but instead of receiving help, I was fired. A lot of big businesses say that they have an "open door policy" and that people are encouraged to speak to the higher ups or managers if they feel like they need to talk about something personal. Like my experience and other people's, you could face injustice, punishment or repercussions for speaking out. I have also seen in the Military, Soldiers being treated differently and looked at differently for admitting they struggled with PTSD and Depression. The stigma about Mental Health and Addiction is very real in the world and sometimes it is just too painful to think that you will be judged or looked at as a "weak" person, or "crazy", or even being labeled as a "junkie" in some cases.

That goes for our family and friends also. A lot of times they just don't get it and we are just too afraid to be judged or looked at like we are "crazy." I experienced this for many years, trying to convince myself, my family, and even friends that nothing was wrong and I had it "all under control." I am here to tell you, that is absolutely a bad idea regardless of the stigma. Another truth that I know from my experience is that we hate to believe that we are "messed up" or "broken." You need to understand that accepting your mental health does not mean that you accept that you are messed up or mentally broken, or you need to be fixed somehow. It just means that you know you need help and you are ready for change. Remember, it is ok to have problems in your life, you might be struggling with mental health, addiction, lack of value, suicidal thoughts or something else, but whatever it is you must accept it. You will not grow mentally if you continue to focus on the things that you cannot change.

You must only focus on the things you can change. You need to know that you are not alone in this fight. If you are a Combat Veteran or just someone who has experienced a traumatic event, fact is for most of us, we are not the same people. Something in us changes. We do not always know right away what exactly it is, but we know something does not feel right anymore. A lot of the time it is our families and friends that first notice something different about us and usually can tell us what they feel is different. I know my wife and my mother could. The truth is, it may be something

ACCEPTANCE

minor or it could be something big. or unfortunately, it could be everything about you has changed. It really depends on what kind of traumatic event you might have been through. A few examples might be the lack of self-value, personality, or the way you talk, act and think. Traumatic events can happen from thousands of different ways. Here are some of the most common ways outside of combat, car accidents, sexual assault, gun shot, armed robbery, near death experience, or the loss of a child. There are so many traumatic events that happen to people every day and it affects us all differently. Most of the time after something traumatic happens, we find ourselves being diagnosed with mental health conditions like PTSD, Depression and Anxiety.

Remember, the most important thing you need to do is face it, accept it, and start trying to move forward with a positive mindset. Another major reason people fail and never make it to the next level is because they cannot accept what has happened and cannot admit they are struggling. That is when denial will destroy your mindset, relationships and friendships. That is why Acceptance is so important, because you cannot move on to the next level of your life without doing so. For many years, I could not accept that my family was suffering because of my mental health and addiction. I never understood how bad I was hurting my family and in how many ways. Sometimes it gets hard for us once we realize all the pain that we have caused to those we love because of our denial and not willing to get the help that was needed. Like the 22 Veterans every day, I wanted to end my life instead of accepting what has happened. It can be scary once you have "woken up" and see the truth with your own eyes. You see all the pain you have caused people and it hurts, but remember, your family and friends love you and want to see you grow, so now is the time to start facing the truth, and accept your reality so that you can move forward. Once you have done that, it gives space to start focusing on your new mission and your new mindset.

For me in my situation I had to first accept that I was struggling with my mental health and my addiction. Second, I accepted that I needed help. Third, I had to accept the fact it was only going to get better with hard work. Fourth, I just had to do what it took. Once I started to take these steps and apply them to my life, everything changed for me, and now I am here today living my best life because of those steps. I have also changed my mindset during the process. You can do the same if you are disciplined. You can either give up and watch your life continue in the same way it's been, or you can accept it, face it, and kick its ass! As soon as you decide to defeat your situations, start building up a positive mentality, and really start thinking and believing that you are going to win and be successful at everything you do, you will start seeing the changes happen. Those changes will motivate you more because you are seeing the results that you desire.

Trust me, I know it's not easy to always accept the hard times in our life. There are millions of people that live their whole life never accepting anything that has happened to them; from childhood trauma to adult trauma. It is always easier just to tell yourself, "Not to think about it," and just live your life without ever addressing anything you had ever

ACCEPTANCE

gone through. Sadly, that's a huge part of the problem of why we lose on average 22+ Veterans every day from suicide, because they don't know how to deal with any Traumatic Event, Mental Health issues, or Addictions. I have seen it time and time again where a Veteran would isolate themselves and give up before they will ask for help. There are many reasons why Veterans, and men in particularly, feel this way because of the "Stigma" that is surrounded around PTSD, Depression and Anxiety.

For many years, I have talked about how the stigma is a lie and it's destroying men. It started back in the days when people expected men not to have emotions. Men had to be strong 24/7 and show zero emotions. When it comes to the military, they still teach you that you have to put your emotions in check and "Man Up," and I agree to a certain level to that. Only if you are in the Active Military and you are on a combat mission, must you put whatever you are going through on the back burner or talk with a Chaplin or a "battle buddy." You must take care of your man on the right and the man of the left of you. But you must always put the mission first. And you can't do that if you don't take care of yourself first like we discuss earlier. It is even harder when it comes to the Active Military, because in the Military, you are taught to be strong, to be a leader, and you must be "Combat Ready" for a mission at all times. It is still your responsibility to get the help that is needed when you are struggling, but when you are told you are weak because you need help, it makes you not want to ask for it. That is why I worked so hard to stop the stigma. The fact is that it is harder for a man and most Veterans to admit they are struggling and one reason I try so hard to prove to them that

I am strong even though I struggle with Mental Health. There is nothing worse than losing a fellow battle buddy because they were too embarrassed to ask for help.

Remember this, accepting your situation is vital to recovering. You must not only accept it, but you must be open with it to others, including yourself. I don't mean broadcast it to the world, but do not be ashamed. We all have some type of issues from a mental disability, physical disability, to some type of addiction. The important fact you need to understand is that you are not alone. When you share your story with others, not only will you help someone, but you give others hope. You will see that others will relate with you and that will help give you the confidence to keep moving forward. Accepting what has caused the struggles in your life in the first place is a huge gain. Once you "accept what is what," now you learn to focus on the next chapter. Focus on how to deal with your current situations. One of the biggest strategies that helped me was when I started to accept the fact that I was an opioid addict. When I chose to accept my addiction, it opened other options for me. I started getting help to address the addiction. What else is great about Acceptance is that once you start to address these addictions, it will start highlighting other areas of your life that you need to deal with, like the fact that you cannot continue to blame yourself for everything bad that happens even if whatever happens was because of bad choices you made. Taking responsibility for those choices is most important, but also you must forgive yourself for, too.

ACCEPTANCE

If you don't stop hating and blaming yourself for everything that is a mess in your life right now, you will never get past the Acceptance phase. Some people might accept that they have an issue, but they don't take responsibility and focus on how to change it. So, until you start focusing on what you can change today, you will never start the healing process. You will learn more in depth later in this book about forgiving yourself for what has might of have caused other's pain. You see, you cannot start the process of healing until you accept "why" you have the issues. Whatever the reasons are that have made you the way you are, just know, there is nothing wrong with you. You should always love yourself. That is another big part of Acceptance; accepting your conditions and situations, but accepting the "You," the REAL you. Loving yourself and caring for yourself means you want change.

Don't forget that this is not no easy journey. A friend once told me "The more you invest in yourself, the better the return will be." You will soon see that the harder something is to do, the more it will be worth it when accomplished. If you are the kind of person that always cuts corners and does things the easy way, then you will probably struggle with this. There are no short cuts when it comes to personal development. You get out what you put in. The harder you work, the better the results. It's so true what people say; "hard work pays off." I am proof of that. When I first started to get my life in order I wanted to give up. It was too hard to stay on track, and some days I almost did, but I knew that I wanted to have a better life, better than I had been living for the last 10 years. I had to keep motivating myself any way I could. That is why I created this book so that you had something to guide you when you start feeling the same way I did. Read this book as many times as it takes to get you back into the "Go Mode" mentality. You are the only one that can stop yourself from success at upgrading your mindset to a 2.0 version.

Start today by working on accepting your past. It is what it is and you cannot change it. Accept what is your current situation accepting any mental health, family struggles, relationships, or addictions that you might be struggling with currently. Now that you have accepted what your situations are and what needs to be done, and how to get it done, be excited for a new future. Stay positive in knowing your life is going to get better in so many ways. Every day, wake up ready to begin your new journey. Start with your meditations or Affirmations and tell yourself you will not be beaten down or consumed by your mental health problems any longer! Today will be a great day because you have everything under control. Plan your weekly goals and execute them. Believe in yourself and make the changes needed. You can no longer focus on the old you. Remember, you cannot change your past, but you can change your future. You are growing into the person who has always been there. You just lost track of them. Be proud that you are stepping up and doing this for yourself. It is not an easy task to accept the bad things that have happened or the bad situations you might be in right now. That is why in the end, you will be so much happier because you will prove to yourself, and any doubters, how strong you really are.

ACCEPTANCE

There is not much more I can tell you when it comes to Acceptance. I have made it pretty clear on what it is you need to do and how you will need to do it. Again, it will take time to get you to the 2.0 Mindset, but you are on your way to being in Recovery. Remember, as soon as you decide you are ready for change, the change will begin. The next chapter is vital for Acceptance to work in your life. You must focus on the changes you want started. You will soon see how each lesson comes together, and as we continue, I will show you why you can't grow without each one of these lessons.

CHAPTER

3

Focus

In this chapter, we will discuss the importance of Focus. You will now understand why the last chapter you read on Acceptance is so important before moving on. I will show you how they work together and why you cannot work on one without mastering the other. This is the 3rd phase to the next level. I believe this is important in many ways and that you will soon understand why. As for myself, it is still one of my biggest challenges I face today. If we are being honest with each other, I am sure most of you reading this right now would agree that focusing on one task is a huge challenge in your life, as well. Think about it; with everything going on in this world right now, it is incredibly hard to focus on one thing. Am I right? Have you ever wished you could concentrate on more than just one thing? Have you ever wished that you could focus more on just your mission or your goals? I know I have. That is why we are going to discuss this third step to a 2.0 Mindset.

Focusing on everything that is important in your life right now and learning how to focus on upgrading your mindset is the key.

Understand this, before you can start to focus on your new mission, task, or even goals, you must read and learn the first two chapters of this workbook. You must understand that once you are in the right mindset learning to accept what is, and what was, before any of this, now matters in your life. Now that you are starting Chapter 3, you will understand more about Focus. You will start understanding so much clearer and see things the way I do. You need to understand that after you have made the decision that you are ready for a positive change and you want to create a growth mindset, you have to master Acceptance. Not only with your past, but also today. Just like any of these other steps you have learned with everything in life, if you want to be great at something you must practice. Learning to focus is no different, it takes hard work, time, and patience.

I have found from my own experience that most of the time we jump past the Acceptance stage and go straight into the Focus stage without even thinking about it. We get in the right mindset, but we start to focus on whatever comes to our mind first. We build up the motivation to get started and then we create this "Let's get it" attitude and mindset. This is normal for Veterans since we have been trained to have that "get up and go" mentality once we are tasked with a mission. One of the best things about being in the Army is we put a lot time into strategies and planning before we execute a mission. I will tell you this, planning is the most time consuming, but it is the most important.

Instead of proper planning, I have seen most people just jump right into their ideas. That may not sound so bad to the average person who is motivated and ready to work, but when you do it without any plans or strategies, it is not such a good idea. You see, most people do it without thinking about it. Why? It is normal for those people that have not reached a 2.0 mindset, because they never think about any kind of steps to take first to build a successful life or mindset. Everything they do in life is with an unconscious mindset. I know this because I lived that way for a long time. The only way to get out of being unconscious is to wake up and start being more conscious with your life.

That is why this workbook is so important for your personal development and mindset. Believing and learning the process is key, and doing it right, your life will change. What I tell people often is, "Remind yourself that you are a human and nobody is perfect." No matter how far you get, you will never achieve perfection. You can become a professional at whatever you want, but you will never become a perfect human being. That is just the way it is. You will always make mistakes and that is ok. You must accept it and move on. Now, like I said earlier, people with a basic mindset will skip the Acceptance stage and just focus on ideas that sound good in the moment hoping they can make changes by just trying something new or doing something somebody told them to do. Unfortunately, that usually never works out. One of the major reasons why is because eventually, you will still have to face those same mental health problems or any addictions you have struggled with. Remember, your problems do not just disappear. They will never just go away. You might forget them for a little while and push them down into your subconscious mind, but they will always be there.

There are also many people that are too impulsive. Those types of people are call impromptu. They do not use any strategies or plans to reach their goals. They just go with the flow without thinking about it and have the attitude of "let's see what happens." If you are that type of person, you will need to really focus on this workbook because if you do not have any plans, solutions, or strategies to execute your goals, most likely it will not work out. The fact is, if you start working towards your goal and you have no idea how to achieve them, and you skip steps like Acceptance, you get reckless and you start making many mistakes, including like I said earlier, continuing to struggle with the same problems, eventually, as most of you may have already figured out, those problems get worse the longer you ignore them. So, you must address your situations and get it right before you can move forward. However, there are many reasons why we avoid facing our issues. Trust me, I know far too well.

I have avoided many things in my life and I just could not accept certain things in my past, like combat traumatic events, loss of my best friend to suicide, relationships, addictions, and my mental health. I finally learned after many years of suffering that if you do not accept the things that have hurt you in the past or the things that have been holding you down now, you will never be able to move forward or start focusing on your mission or goals. It took me many years to understand that, and once I did, my life began to change for the better. You need to first figure out what your goals are, and what it is that you want to do or get better at. You need to find a solution that will help you get there in the most effective way possible. Whatever it is that you decide to work on, you need to start focusing on it right now. I am going to assume that building a Veteran Mindset 2.0 is something that you are wanting to do, and if I am correct, then this workbook needs to be the number one focus in your life right now. It is important to focus on each of these tasks one at a time, it will help you be much more productive and help you get it done correctly. Think about what you are struggling with the most right now. Are you struggling more with your Mental Health? Are you struggling with Addiction?

Maybe it is your unhealthily mindset that is hurting you the most. Think about each one of these and the other things that are going on in your life and decide which one to start focusing on right now. I have also learned from my own experiences that if you do not face and accept what is happening in your life right now, then how can you ever move forward? You must start facing and accepting the situations that you are struggling with. The other thing is you must stop the multitasking. Focus on that one thing that is most important, and get it done. If changing your mindset is your priority, that needs to be your only focus right now. You must put all your energy into it. That is how you will develop the 2.0 Mindset. There are many ways to help you learn to focus better. Some of the things I found to help me with focusing were focus groups on social media. There are also meet up groups in or around your area. You can now also create zoom calls with people that have some of the same issues as you, start discussions, and talk about different ideas and ways to help each other. Surrounding yourself with people that want the same thing is a blessing. If you struggle with addiction, going to AA and NA meetings are also another way to help you focus on your mission. If your goals are to get clean and sober or to build fellowships, those are great places to start. You can also talk with professionals like life coaches and councilors that provide services that will teach you how to focus with meditations, yoga, and therapy. There are many reasons why focusing can be so hard to do, especially when dealing with mental health issues like PTSD, ADHD, Depression and Anxiety. It can feel so impossible at times. I struggled for so long with all those things that I could not find one thing that I could stay focused on to the end. I would jump around from one thing to the other constantly because either I would lose interest or I would lose focus on my task. It has always been a struggle for me, ever since I was a child struggling with ADHD. That is why I would never finish any projects or tasks that I started because I could not focus on anything long enough to finish it. Through practice and dedication, I forced myself to do what was needed to reach my goals. One thing that I still do not do, unless it is absolutely necessary, is multitask.

I understand that in today's world, multitasking is pretty normal and is something that we must learn to do at certain times. Only multitask on the things that need to get done because your daily job and family life require it. Trying to manage work and home life can be stressful and most of us have no choice but to multitask. When it comes to life and family you may need to do it once in a while, but when it comes to your own personal development and building up your mindset, multitasking is a big mistake. You probably have already realized that when you try to focus on a bunch of things at once, it just stresses you out more, and it limits your ability with productivity and the quality of your work. So, with that said, it is definitely something you should not do often. Focusing on one thing at a time will help you more in the long run. You must focus on today's mission and today's goals. Here is an example about how much focus went into writing this book. For many months, I had to focus only on one thing at a time and put all my energy into this. I had to isolate myself and block out the outside world, of course, only at writing times.

Every day, you need to create some time that you can focus on your task, picking a time during the day that is best for you. You do not want to try to focus on your task when there's a distraction present. I know that sounds like common sense, but you would be surprised by how many people try to concentrate while in a room full of chaos. Another great way to start practicing focus is to start working out. Forcing yourself to exercise and getting your blood flowing is extremely good for you for many reasons. Health is the obvious reason, but before you start your task and getting your ideas to start coming more often, you need to be active and doing a short workout that could really help you. It also helps you be more creative and productive and feel better while you work on your goals. Another way to help you is to get plenty of rest. A rested mind is a healthy mind and a healthy mind helps you develop more positive thoughts. So, it is very important to get plenty of sleep so you can function and be able to focus at your full potential. The feeling of being tired is one of the major reasons people give up on the things they need to work on. "I will get it tomorrow," "I will get to it later." These are usually the results from not being well rested and feeling lazy.

Also, never allow the negativity around you to stop you from reaching your goal. We let too many things stop us when we focus too much on the negativity around us. I tell people all the time that we are emotional human beings and bad things do happen daily. If not every single day, at least some point in your life, bad things are going to happen. When those bad days happen, it will be up to you to decide on how you handle those situations. Every situation is different, but you still need to try to focus on the positive side of things, if possible. Remember, having an unhealthy mindset means you probably live an unhealthy life as well. That lifestyle choice comes with so much negativity that it feels impossible to focus on anything good in your life. Here are some examples that you might have struggle with, with an unhealthy mindset during a bad situation. Through my experiences, the first thing is that you get angry and start having negative thoughts. Then usually if you are doing a task and it does not go your way, you want to give up and quit on your goals. Maybe you start to blame the world for all your problems. You start to focus on all the wrong things, and when we do that, it starts to create more problems because your negative attitude and your negative reactions to the bad days is what creates more negative bad days.

You must focus on the things that are good in your life. The more you focus on the good things, the more good days will happen, and the more productivity happens with your goals. This is the reason focus is so important in so many ways. You must focus not only on the good things but focus on your mission, health, and your mindset. I put this information in this workbook because I honestly believe that if you live it and breathe it, you will take your focus to the next level. There are many challenges that Veterans struggle with that play a huge factor on why focusing can seem impossible. Mental Health challenges are the most common. Here are some examples that I have struggled with and I know many of you are struggling with also. ADHD and PTSD are the most common. I had trouble with my mind wondering off and daydreaming when I was trying to write this book. I know many others have these same issues and some even more severe.

I am proof that if you put the work in that it can be achieved. Once you finish whatever you are working on, you will feel so much better about yourself. Your confidence will grow and so will your self-esteem. Once that happens, it makes it so much easier to focus on your achievements and the things that make you feel good. When you can start doing that, it will help you become better prepared for the next mission. Remember, you must create your own environment. You must create positivity all around you. You must understand that you create your own happiness. That is why poor people can be happy and why rich people can be miserable, because it is not just one thing makes us happy. You must focus and create your happiness i.e., family, friends, life, or grateful to be alive. Take in the fresh air. Be appreciative and grateful to be able to simply get up and put your shoes on to go for a walk. Be grateful that you can go outside. Be grateful that you can get into your car and go anywhere you choose. There is so much left to be grateful for no matter what you have lost or what you have been through. These are all things that help us learn to focus on the right stuff in our lives. That is what a 2.0 Mindset is about, focusing on the greater things in life, and changing the way you look at your life and the things around you. It's about learning to focus on everything that makes your life good.

Your mindset is so powerful! Think about it like this, if you are the type of person who believes they have had a miserable life and has never had anything good happen to them, you will always think that way until you look at it differently. It is not only the situations you have been through in your life that has continued to make you miserable, but it is also because of all the negative reactions you have had towards those situations. Your negative mindset has been created because of all the lack of positivity which has been controlling you all these years. It has been creating chaos and you probably never realized you could have stopped a lot of your pain and anger just by changing your thought process and mindset. Things in your life will start to work the same way once you change to a positive mindset. Once you change it into a 2.0 Mindset, you will start to believe, love and care about things and people so much more.

If you want to see more great things happen, you must believe with more positivity, and good things will start happening more often. That is how powerful our mindset is. This concept blew me away once I realized how powerful our minds are. The power of our mindset is so strong that it controls our life with happiness, sadness, and anger, and we manifest the things that happen. You are in control and you choose how your life is. I will remind you that we cannot control everything that happens but we can control how we react during those bad days. There is no denying that the bad days will still come. I never want you to forget that and I will never tell you that once you take your mindset to a 2.0 level that you will only have the best life never experiencing bad days again. That is not what I am telling you. The fact is you will see bad days again and you may even experience another traumatic event. You might even lose a loved one. That is just how life works. Ultimately, there is a higher power that controls all. We all have a purpose and reason why we were created and sometimes God's plan is something we do not understand, but through much prayer and meditation, we can find our purpose. Remember, you still have free will, and you can control what roads you take to reach your destination.

You control the decisions that you make. Nobody forces you to do the things you do or act the way you act. You can go or you can stay home. You can do it or not, the choice is yours. One of my favorite examples I like to give is this; your life is like a deck of cards. We cannot control the cards we are dealt. The hand we get is not our choice, but we do control how we chose to play those cards. We make the decision if we want to fold or go for it. It is a game of chance and skill knowing the odds that are against you and understanding the risk. Remember, if you go for it, you just might beat the odds and win it all. Or you could go for it and lose it all. Life happens, but what is most important is that you keep trying. You might lose a couple of times and you might win other times. It is about how much focus and determination you put in. Remember, all successful people have lost plenty of times. You cannot win without losing occasionally. So, go for it and if you fail and you walk away and never play again, then that is the choice you made.

If you lose and you react to it in a positive way, look at it as a lesson learned and you try again, that is also your choice. You can also fold and not even try. Remember by giving up and not trying you automatically fail. The point I am making here is that if you want to upgrade your mindset, focus on the positivity in your life. Focus on your mission today. You can achieve so much greatness just by focusing on what matters and doing what needs to be done. You must stay consistent and you must do what needs to be done every single day. Once you start focusing on your mission, your life will start changing. Only then will you be ready for the next level of your mindset and begin to start knowing what your self-worth is all about.

CHAPTER 4

Self-Worth

Before we dive right into this chapter, I want you to understand that I believe that self-worth is one of the most important lessons you will learn in this book. No matter how far you get in your transition to a 2.0 Mindset, learning your own self-worth is something that will change your life forever and will help you grow into a much better person no matter what your goals are. Let's first start off by learning the true definition of "Self-Worth" and what it means. We define Self-Worth as having awareness of knowing one's own value or worth as a person. Having an opinion of yourself, believing if you are a good person and deserve good things, or believing you are a bad person and deserve bad things, are examples. Self-Worth is all about how you feel about yourself. Just knowing that, you should understand how important it is when deciding your self-worth. Knowing how valuable you are is huge in your recovery stage. Another point I want to discuss about "Self-Worth" is that not only does it play a huge role in your transition to a 2.0 Mindset, but I like to call it the "Master of the Self-Words." What I mean is this, the word (self) comes in many forms and definitions. For example, Self-Confidence, Self-Esteem, Self-Love, and Self-Respect, etc. These are all "self-words" and I believe that most of these types of self-words can be combined together and be listed under the "Master Word" of Self-Worth. If you do not have Self-Worth, then you cannot have any of the other "self-words" in your life. If you know your self-worth, then most likely, you are in a great place and do not struggle with any of the other ones. Now that you have a better understanding about Self-Worth, how it works, and how important it is, let me tell you about my experience with my own self-worth and how I have come to the conclusion that learning to have Self-Worth has changed my life. For many years, I had no idea what my worth was, what it looked like, or what it even meant. I had no idea how important believing in myself was or understanding how much self-worth I had, and the truth is, for a long time, my life was falling apart. I was not only destroying myself but I was destroying everything around me.

A new life started when I decided to make changes to get where I felt I needed and truly wanted to be, to become a better man. So, I started to learn what Self-Worth was and I started changing my outlook, not just in my life, but everything around me and how I could use it to help me become successful. After using the first three steps of this book, I finally found my self-worth again and I knew I was made for greatness. That is when everything got better, for not just me, but my family and those around me. Once you learn to love yourself and believe in yourself, you become a happier person taking yourself to a whole new level and you become more enjoyable to be around. You bring positive energy to all those around you. You will soon understand all this once you start changing the way you feel about yourself. Once you realize how much value you actually have, your life will begin to change. Your behavior, your actions, and your decisions will soon reflect off your own thoughts of how you feel about yourself. You need to learn exactly who you are as a person. You need to know why you are the way you are. You need to understand yourself, love yourself, and care for yourself. If you want to get to a 2.0 Mindset and be successful in life then you need to learn all this and more. Why would anyone invest or believe in you if you do not believe in yourself? One of the main reasons we are losing so many Veterans to suicide is because they have no idea that they are worth so much more than they feel.

A lot of Veterans that come out of combat feel this way. They feel numb to the world and feel like nobody understands them anymore. Believe me, we all want to be loved and cared for, but it feels almost impossible because of the life we had to live. Many Veterans come out the Military after struggling with traumatic events. Many of the actions they take and events they see has led to mental health disorders like, PTSD, Depression, Anxiety, and even Addiction. Remember, many Veterans have been to combat multiple times and have learned to stay in "Combat Mode" always ready for the next mission. One of the biggest problems I speak about is that the Military taught us to turn on the "Kill Switch" and get into "Combat Mode" but they don't teach you how to turn it off. That is why so many of us do not make it after military life because we do not know how to adjust and get to that Veteran Mindset 2.0, until now, with this book's help.

Right now, you might be struggling with PTSD, Depression, or maybe you are just struggling with hope and purpose. Maybe you are struggling with loving yourself. Maybe you are tired of failing and just want to give up. I was there for almost 10 years of my life. Even today, I still struggle. Remember the first step, look back to the first chapter in this book (Mindset). That is the first step to Recovery. Right now, you are in a different mentality and that is ok, because once you have accepted your situation, you will begin to open up a path to knowing your self-worth again and continuing the path to recovery which leads to changing your mindset. I always remind Veterans and people in general that the fact you are struggling with PTSD, Depression, or any kind of mental health problems is that you are going to have issues. It's common to fight with yourself about certain difficulties, whether it's a physical or a mental disability, it is still hard to deal with. The truth is that no matter the situation you are in if you decide to make positive changes and stick with it, something is going to change inside of you and it's going to change your life.

Even when you make it out of this black hole you're fighting, you are going to have struggles. The difference is that you will remember how to get back. One of the things that I learned throughout my struggles is that even a man with no legs and no arms will find a way to live life again if they choose to. Somebody with a brain disability or somebody that has mobility issues still has a choice to live. Learning to

SELF-WORTH

live with your disability is a huge part of getting to Recovery. You must understand that even though you are struggling with a disability, that disability does not define who you are as a person. You are not your disability and your disability, is not you! Knowing your self-worth is going to play an important role in that, because if you know how much value you have, you won't describe yourself with PTSD, Depression, Anxiety, or any other issues. It is ok to recognize that you have a disability but never allow it to define you.

I want to discuss another "self-word" and that is, Self-Care. I see so many Veterans that come back from combat and they just do not take care of themselves anymore. Most of them start drinking or self-medicate just to deal with the events they are struggling with. I've talk to them and most do not even get help because they feel like the VA can't help them. So, they do not even try. A large portion of them don't even have benefits at the VA. Sometimes, it takes years to get into the system and that is why it is important to show our brothers and sisters that us Veterans that have made it past our struggles, need to be there for them and show them there is a way to get better. I have been down that road many times as well, and if you are the person reading this and you don't believe in yourself anymore or you don't feel like you're worth anything, please understand that you are not alone. Millions of us feel or have felt this way. There are many of reasons that Veterans struggle with mental health, and it's not just "Combat Veterans" that struggle, there are many different reasons. For example, you may struggle with PTSD, Anxiety, loss of hope, depression or have suicidal thoughts. I know of

Veterans that got pulled out of the Military because of injuries, mentally and physically, and truthfully, those are the worst because I lived that life, so I can relate. I was rounding up halfway through my second tour when I injured myself on a mission. I jumped off a MRAP during a dismount mission and I landed wrong and tore my ACL and a partial tear of my meniscus. So long story short, I got sent to FT. Gordon for surgery and ended up spending two years there being medically retired, because even though I was there for surgery, I was told I was no longer deployable because I was being diagnosed with PTSD with Psychosis and Major Depression, among many other mental health issues I was struggling with. With everything going on, I was now being told within six months that I had to accept that my military career was over. That was the beginning of eight long years of hell. It took me eight years to finally reach out and get the help I needed. Once I woke up and realized that I controlled my own destiny, my life started to change. I found purpose again and my self-worth.

What changed is that I no longer allowed my mental health to define me and I started giving myself the self-care that was needed so that I could help others. Self-Care is something you must do for you. You must keep building yourself up and know your worth. You must start believing in yourself again, because nobody out here in this big world is going to believe in you if you do not believe in yourself, first. We all know this is not a nice world and things are not always fair. So, if you want something in life, you have to go get it. Live with no more excuses!

Another way I learned to find my self-worth is to ask yourself these three questions:

1. Who am I at my core?

2. What am I struggling with?

3. What do I want in life?

Ask yourself these three questions. Answer them honestly because if you never understand who you are, what you are struggling with, and what you really want, then you will never get to the next phase in your life. You will never upgrade to a 2.0 Mindset. Once you have answered those three questions, study them and reread them over and over. Remind yourself on bad days what you want and what it takes to achieve it. Use them as notes to remind yourself of how far you have come and how far you want to go. There are many of ways to help cope with mental health and addictions. You can learn different exercises and methods to achieve greatness. This book is a guide to do just that, to get you to a level you have never been before. Do what needs to be done and study this book, especially the practicals section and questions at the end. If you take this seriously, you will start living your best life. You can make positive changes just by following these steps that you are learning now. Focus on these lessons that you are learning and all you will need to do is apply them to your life. Always keep positive people around you at all times, negativity can change a weak mind instantly. There are toxic people everywhere and they do not want to see us succeed which is why staying focused on your mission is so important. Never allow the negativity of others to distract you from your goals. There will be times you will feel like giving up, so when that happens, reread this book and go back over everything you read or go over the three answers that you wrote down. When surrounded by negativity, it is always best to focus on anything that is positive. Remember, understand that your self-worth and the opinions of others do not affect you. You have come this far and now there is no going back. You know what it takes now to get yourself to the top of your game. No more excuses! This is going to be the most difficult challenge you have ever had to take on, because it is not just a physical challenge, it is a mental challenge, too. That is why once you get the results you want, it will be the most rewarding. Remember, anything in life that is hard it is usually worth it. If it was easy then everyone could do it and there would be no problems in the world, but it's not. Since you have decided to get your mindset on the right track and realize how much value your life holds, it's time to start preparing for Recovery. This is your time, and nobody can take that from you, only you can do that. The next chapter you read will bring everything you have learned thus far together and you will get a better understanding of what Recovery is. I hope to motivate you to keep pushing forward in Chapter Five.

CHAPTER

5

Recovery

Welcome to Chapter 5, Recovery. Congrats on making it this far! This is the last chapter of this workbook. I am so excited that you have made it here but remember, this is far from over. You have the practicals and the workbook questions remaining plus the actual work that you need to do. So, the reading of the chapters may come to an end but the work is far from over. Get ready for the real work that is just beginning, because now we will take everything you have learned in the first four chapters and put them all together. This is how you get into the Recovery Phase. You are now in the beginning stage of transitioning into a 2.0 Mindset and you can only do that by successfully completing each chapter, reading the practicals, and applying everything you learned into your life. The first thing we will talk about is what exactly does Recovery mean. It is important to remember that recovery in this book may not mean the same thing like in other situations. The Recovery phase here does not mean you are cured. Recovery means that you have learned coping skills, strategies, and techniques to live a healthy upgraded 2.0 Mindset with Mental Health conditions. We will focus and work on all 5 areas of your life to ensure you are staying on the right path to success. Let me remind you of the 5 areas we need to continue to focus on so that you stay in the Recovery Phase.

- Physically
- Mentally
- Emotionally
- Spiritually
- Financially

You must always stay focused on each one of these areas with the lessons that you have learned. If you do then you will continue to the top of your game with a 2.0 Mindset.

Each one of those major areas play a vital role in your life. It is important to always stay focused. When you find yourself in a battle, figure out which one of the five areas you are struggling with and use this workbook to help you get through it. It is important to remind yourself that just because you are in the recovery stage that you don't get complacent. You will have bad days and there will be times that you will be tested. It is important to always stay on the right path and stay focused on your mission. Always remind yourself of the reasons why you wanted to grow mentally and emotionally. Always pay attention to your Mind, Body and Soul. These are also vital to your success, mindset, and your health. Here are three examples of what they are and what role they play.

1. Mind - our soul projecting itself mentally

2. Body - our soul projecting itself physically

3. Soul - a pre-manifested energy and encompasses of the Body, Mind and Emotions.

Each one of these are important to having a healthy life and mindset. Even if 2 out of 3 are doing good, you will find yourself in a bad place. You need to be focused and in sync with all three. I found thus out the hard way many times. You will learn many examples and techniques on how you can get all three in the right place later on in this book. It is also important to understand that there will be days that you will not feel like working on yourself but just remember that we all go through that. You are not alone in this. I still find days that my depression kicks in and it tries to consume me and bring me down. Sometimes it takes a couple days for me now to get myself back up and going. The most important task is to make sure you get back up! It is like when you are in recovery from alcohol or drugs and you have been clean for a while but all those negative thoughts start to kick in and tries to get you to relapse. That is how some mental health conditions work, even though you feel better and you find yourself growing, you still have the PTSD, Depression, Anxiety, and even Addiction, lingering around in your subconscious mind just waiting for an invitation to consume you again.

Another important factor is to make sure you are engaging with positive family and friends. Surrounding yourself around good people is a great way to keep yourself in a good mindset. It can be hard at times with all the negativity going on, but you have to do your best. Those that do know me, know that I am on all the social media platforms trying to get my message out to the community and so I am constantly running into negative comments and people daily. It is challenging some days, but I must remind myself how far I have come, so I stay focused on my message. As long as I continue to focus on the positivity, the easier it will be to stay in recovery. Never lose your focus. Another way I look at staying in recovery is like this; you must start making positive things happen, and start focusing on the kind of future you want. You must stop looking back on those things that were traumatic in your life. You will never forget the bad things that have happened, but once you are in full recovery and have upgraded your mindset, you will have the ability to move forward and no longer allow your past to stop you or control you. The sad truth is, majority of Veterans that are struggling with mental health conditions will give up and quit because they cannot deal with the things that happened to them or the things they have seen. That is why the suicide rate is so high, because people in general will not ever learn how to stop focusing on the bullshit in their life or in the past.

That is why this book is so important, because I am teaching people that their mindset is so powerful that it literally controls everything we do, how we feel about ourselves, and how we live and treat others. Change your mindset and you will change your life. You must want to change and be willing to do whatever it takes to get there. There are many ways to help you face your issues. Here is the most common way that I teach others and it worked for me in the beginning. You must stand up to your mental health conditions. You must face them and kick its ass! Go to a room with a mirror and look at yourself and really focus deep inside. Dive right in and tell your conditions the deal:

"Hear me Depression," "Hear me PTSD," "Hear me Anxiety,"

"I struggled for a long time with you, and I have let you consume my life long enough. I will no longer allow you to control my life! I know my self-worth, I know my life matters, and I am ready to move forward without you. I will no longer allow you to control my life."

Trust me, this might sound crazy talking to yourself and calling out your problems like this, but I promise you that I have done this technique more times than I remember and it has worked. I have looked at myself in the mirror and told myself daily just to remind myself that I would not give up and I would not quit. This is part of the self-care process and you will learn more about those kinds of affirmations and techniques in the practicals section. Another way you can look at it is to think about that Veteran or the person that is struggling with some type of addiction. It can be any kind of Addiction like drugs, pornographic videos, gambling, alcohol, or maybe it is all of them or just one addiction. Either way, imagine that person trying to make it to the end of their treatment, and they get to the last page of the AA/NA book of 12-steps. They get all the way through the final steps and treatments and they are told they are still an addict. Why? It's because even though they are clean and sober, they still need to learn how to heal from being a drug addict, or an alcoholic, so they do not relapse. That is how recovery works.

This is the same concept you are learning here in this book. You are now learning how to heal from your traumatic events, or maybe, you are learning how to heal from a destructive mindset and suicidal thoughts. Whatever your reason is for wanting changes in your life, you must learn how to recover from it. You are learning new ways to move forward without those things in your life. That is what recovery is here. If you do what you are supposed to do and focus on the right things, you may not be cured from your mental health issues, your traumatic events, or addictions, but you are learning new ways to live your life by upgrading your mindset. It is important to use each lesson step-by-step in this book the way it is written. The five lessons you have learned will take you where you need to go. If you are struggling from PTSD because of a traumatic event in your life, you must start healing if you ever want to live happy and successful. You must take your life back by no longer living in the past.

Get yourself to that point where you no longer look back on those things that have happened, because now, you are fully focused on your future. I am so proud of you! I am sure that you will begin seeing changes in your life as soon as you start applying the lessons, techniques, and coping skills you will learn in this book. Once you feel like you are at that point you are finally recovered, you will want to start sharing your story. You will start using the mess in your life as your message. A few years from now when you have other veterans reaching out to you, helping others will be a no brainer for you because giving back is in all of us. Remember to use your experiences to help them to move forward. I also call this Recovery, because even though you are still in recovery from your issues, you have gotten to that place to where you are in control of your life. With you being in control, you can focus on what brings you joy and happiness.

Being happy gives you the ability to help other people that need a boost up because you have been through the struggle, you have been through those suicidal thoughts, you have been through the substance abuse, you have been through the traumatic events. Guess what? You have gotten through it all and now you have a 2.0 Mindset. When that time comes, remind yourself how far you have come and be proud of yourself. Like I said earlier, hard days will come and there will be things that will happen that will test you. As long as you change your thought process and understand that bad things will happen, and that we cannot stop them from happening, you understand that you can get through it. It is all about how you address those bad days. It took me a long time to understand that I cannot control bad days, but I can control how I react to them and how I feel. It is all about the positive and negative energy around you. The more positivity you push out, the more positivity will come in, and vice versa. You react to bad days in a negative way then you will get more negativity back, and more often. That is what having a 2.0 Mindset is all about, upgrading the how you think, and changing your outlook on everything. You no longer look at the problems but focus on the solutions. Another thing to remember is that upgrading your mindset takes time depending on what exactly you are struggling with.

It took me eight years to start thinking differently and it took me one year to write this book. Do not expect yourself to be perfect. You are going to slip up sometimes and say and do things you are not proud of, but what is important is that you recognize it. Always take responsibility for your actions and step up when you know you are in the wrong. When you start learning how to focus before acting out on a situation, you know you are growing. Remember when struggling with PTSD, or Survivor's Guilt, anger is the hardest emotion to get a handle on. Trust me I know. Anger has been my biggest challenge for years. The reason I bring up anger is because after spending years talking with and helping Veterans, I have learned that anger is the number one emotion that most of us struggle with and most of us want to get under control. Again, it will happen, but it takes time. Focus on all your lessons here, and after this chapter, learn the coping skills and techniques that are in this book. Greatness takes time and nothing worth your while comes easy. Do not, I repeat, DO NOT, let others put a time limit on you, not family, friends, or even your spouse. You will upgrade your mindset when you're ready, everyone is different.

Focus on what you are doing and keep working at it. Reread this book as many times as you need to. Nobody can put a time limit on your success. Be proud that you have come this far. Be proud that you are trying to change, because I am. You are an amazing person, and you deserve happiness just like everybody else, but the truth is you have been through a lot and not everybody makes it to this point. Remember what I told you, 22+ Veterans commit suicide every day in America. So, the fact that you are here in this book trying, it says a lot about who you are, whether you are a Veteran or not. You are here at this moment and I am so proud of you. Recovery is about getting passed the struggles that have been holding you down for so long. It might be childhood trauma, or something that happened a few years ago. Everything you have learned, and will learn, in this book will guide you to a 2.0 Mindset if you do what needs to be done. If you treat this like a joke then you will receive a joke result. If you treat this like success then you will get successful results. This is all up to you. I have given you all the tools that I have used to get me to my Recovery.

Upgrading your mindset is not an easy task, but with the right tools and techniques, you can do it. Keep pushing yourself to be the best and never give up just because you do not get the results you want right away. As long as you keep pushing to be the best version of yourself, then you will be. Always remember the "Why." Remind yourself why you want to change and why you are doing this. You can have many motivations to be better, but your reason needs to be for you. Remember, you cannot get through this if you are not doing it for yourself. Just like an addict getting clean, they can get there, but how long will they stay clean doing it for others? If you do it for the right reasons the first time, you do not have to worry about disappointing other people with your progress. Set your limits and take small steps. If you struggle with PTSD and Anxiety then it might take months, or even years, for you to get out in a crowed place. With hard work, dedication, focus, and small steps, you will be able to one day. Everything will happen at the right time. Recovery is not about how fast you get there but about how well you get there. Do not push yourself through the chapters and practicals too fast. All the chapters in this book are short but they are informative. So, take your time and learn as much as you can. Well, what else can I say? You have made it to the end of all five chapters of this book. You will begin the Practicals Section right after this chapter. Congratulations on finishing the five chapters! Now let's go over to the practicals and learn each of these lessons in-depth.

CONCLUSION

Remember I served two tours in Afghanistan and have been struggling with mental health and addiction for 10 years. I have thought about suicide more times than I can count. Today, I have traveled the country speaking on stages, hosting events, and I have built a social media platform with over 50K followers. I have a built a brand that you may have heard of, "Veteran Guy." I am the Owner and Founder of the Veteran Non-Profit Organization, VetLife4Life. I have done things that I have only imagined, including, spending almost an entire year building this workbook for you. The point of telling you this is because I want you to see that you can do anything you put your mind to and as long as you believe in yourself, you can do it! Do not overwhelm yourself, you will reach your 2.0 Mindset when the time is right. It has taken me three years to achieve this level of success. It is important to remind you that the results depend on you. I took everything I have learned through my experiences and put it all into a workbook. I am confident with practice and dedication that you will be just as successful as I am by upgrading you with a Veteran Mindset 2.0.

Everything you have read from Chapter One to Chapter Five lessons will be broken down into key points to help you get a better transition to a 2.0 Mindset. I wanted to give you real examples on how to get yourself into the right mindset and understand each lesson better. Congratulations on getting this far! Remember, you are going to be studying this book, so make sure that you are in the right state of mind and find a quiet place to think. Work on this workbook as much as you can. After you get through the practicals, you will have a section on the back with questions that you can answer, as well as, affirmations for you to study and use. Good luck to you in your future and whatever you do, but never...ever, give up! Remember, after you create your 2.0 Mindset, look out for others and get them a copy of this book. Always pay it forward. I will see you in the Practicals.

THE PRACTICALS

PRACTICALS

Welcome to the practicals section of this book. In these next sections, you will learn more in-depth about everything you have read in the last five chapters. I have taken each of the chapters and broken them down into lessons. Each lesson is broken down so you can understand in-depth exactly how to learn techniques, coping skills, and simply put, how to change your mindset. We will go over all five of the chapters including 10 examples of that lesson.

Mindset

Acceptance

Focus

Self-Worth

Recovery

You have already read my thoughts and experiences on every one of these. Now I will break each one down in-depth for your guide to a Veteran Mindset 2.0.

Mindset

"Turning your Mess into your Message" is just one way I have turned around my mindset. Taking your story and turning them into lessons. There are many ways to accomplish this. Here are some ways I found helpful.

Your Mess Is Your Message

- ➢ Use parts of your life experiences that you have failed at to teach others

- ➢ Use examples of some consequences from bad choices to encourage others

- ➢ Takes parts of your life that you have succeeded at to show others

- ➢ Talk about your story (Books, videos, Audios)

- ➢ Take your story and turn it into a lesson

- ➢ Use any traumatic events that has happened and show how you used it for positivity

- ➢ Write down your story in a journal

PRACTICALS

Affirmations

Creating a positive and healthy mindset takes a lot of practice. There are many ways to do this. One of my most useful ways is by using affirmations daily.

Here are a few that you can use:

- I am good enough
- I am a great person and people love me
- I am a beautiful person on the inside and outside
- I am confident, strong minded, and energized
- I am a successful person, I do great things in my community
- Nobody can stop me from doing what I love, this is my life and I am happy
- I am free of the fear of making mistakes and failure
- I am a positive person and I help people daily to be positive
- I am smart and intelligent and I can do anything

Daily Goals

Set small daily goals by creating stepping stones to gain success, not only in your life, but business. Setting daily goals helps you stay focused and reach accomplishments in your life. It is important to stay on track when you are trying to keep a positive mindset. Setting Goals daily or weekly is up to you. Here are a few that I use to help me:

- Will not lash out at people (control your anger)
- Do not talk down to yourself (disrespect, insults)
- Exercise 30 min daily (walk/run)
- Do your Affirmations every morning
- Give yourself compliments and encourage yourself (Recognize your accomplishments)
- Do something nice for someone every day (Help people out)
- Cut back daily on any bad habits (smoking, cursing, alcohol)
- Do things you enjoy at least a couple times a week. Have fun (parks, friends, travel, family)
- Encourage others to do great things (Humble, Positivity)
- Network with new people (social media)
- Read Motivational books and listen to positive influencers (Tony Robbins, Les Brown, Gary Vaynerchuk)
- Eat more healthy foods (Veggies, smoothies, nuts)

PRACTICALS

Sleep

Sleep is very essential to having a healthy mindset. This took me a long time to release this because I struggle mentally. Once I started to get healthy physically, I still had to find ways to get mentally healthy, as well. Lack of sleep is a huge symptom when struggling with Mental Health. (PTSD, Depression, Anxiety) Here are 10 ideas that I have used to help me get the rest I needed to be productive and get more mentally positive:

- ➢ Have a schedule. Create you a bedtime and a wakeup time even on the weekends (10pm-6am)
- ➢ Avoid taking naps (20 min power naps are ok)
- ➢ Make sure where you sleep is comfortable (mattress/couch)
- ➢ Read a good book an hour before bed
- ➢ Find a bedtime ritual. Meditations or sleep audios are helpful (YouTube/Headspace App)
- ➢ Keep your sleep area cool (60 and 67 degrees)
- ➢ Avoid alcohol, cigarettes, and heavy meals in the late evenings
- ➢ Have sex with your spouse at night before bed (routine)
- ➢ Consult your doctor

➢ Use natural medications

Toxic People

Removing "Toxic" people from your life is a huge key factor to creating a healthy mindset. I have learned many ways to tell if the people around me are toxic and are not good for me. These are the most common signs that you are being affected by toxic people. Here are 15 ways you can identify if you are surrounded by "Toxicity" in your life:

➢ Are the people in your life never supportive and encouraging?

➢ They are very judgmental towards you and others for chasing goals that they do not agree with or understand

➢ Friends that make you defend yourself are not true friends. You should never feel bullied from the people who say they care for you

➢ They never apologize when they are wrong. They never seem to care if they hurt you

➢ Are you emotionally affected by their drama?

➢ Do they make you feel ashamed about yourself? (Negative comments/put you down/make you feel less than them)

➢ Do you dread being around these so called "friends" or feel like you are in fear of them?

PRACTICALS

- Do they always make you prove yourself to them? (Make you feel like you are a liar)

- Do those people in your life ever embarrass you? (Not Jokingly)

- The people you hang out with try to intimidate you to get their way (Guilt trips/Threaten you)

- Are they easily jealous of the things you do or have? (Looks/Clothes/Home/Job/Spouse)

- They constantly see themselves as a victim. They blame everyone and everything for their problems

- They never reach out to check on you. They only call or visit when it benefits them

- Do your friends and family members show up when you need them too?
  (Car problems/rides/babysit/favors)

- Do they get overly defensive when you give them advise? They always feel like you are attacking them for no reason

Getting rid of negative people is one of the most important factors to getting out of toxic relationships. If your environment is surrounded by these types of people, you need to get away now! You are surrounded by Toxicity.

Acceptance

Accepting yourself is the second phase to Recovery. You must learn to accept your reality. Accepting your reality might sound easy enough but many people only accept the reality they choose to see. These next five topics that we will cover will show you the best examples I have mastered through my journey to Recovery:

Accepting Your Reality

- ➢ Accept your reality, good or bad. You must acknowledge it for what it is. You can only change it if you accept it

- ➢ Stop playing it safe. Denial is not your friend. You can't focus on the wrong reality

- ➢ Focus on the now. Set up for future goals but work on your current situations. Focus on today's mission (Mental Health/Addiction/Personal Development)

- ➢ Face your struggles. Get comfortable operating and living there (You cannot hide from your struggles)

- ➢ Let go of your past reality. Focusing on what has been done will not help you move forward. Accepting the past for what it is will help you acknowledge the changes you have made moving forward. (Charlie Mike)

- ➤ Embrace what is unique about you. Acknowledge your strengths and abilities. This act will help build your Self-Confidence

Celebrate Your Accomplishments

Remind yourself that you are an amazing person and that you are great at what you do. Any accomplishments that you have had, big or small, needs to be recognized.
Here are some examples of accomplishments and success you can focus on:

- ➤ Be proud of anything that you have started and finished

- ➤ If you are retired from a job, that is a huge accomplishment. That shows you are reliable and have accepted your responsibilities (Family/Home/Bills)

- ➤ Veteran, Business Owner, Entrepreneur, Financially Successful, and Personal Development are some examples you should always acknowledge

- ➤ Be proud of how far you have come. You have not gotten this far by chance; you made a choice to change. I am proud of you!

- Be grateful for life. You are still breathing, and that means you still possess a chance to live the life you want. You have a purpose to fulfill

- Acknowledge your home life. Always be proud of your children and your spouse's accomplishments, as well. Building others up with positivity will help you in your own self-esteem and self-confidence.

Forgive Yourself

Mental Health conditions and Addictions are a hard reality for most Veterans. When trying to figure it all out, we tend to make many mistakes and hurt people along the way. Too many times in our lives we focus too much on people forgiving us for our wrong doings. You must learn to forgive yourself first. Not everybody will forgive you for things you might have done, and that is ok. Here are some examples why and how you should forgive yourself:

- Forgive yourself and you will be able to move forward in accepting your reality

- Forgiving yourself requires empathy, compassion, kindness, and understanding. These steps are required in all aspects of your life

- No matter how big or minor your mistakes are, you have the right to move forward. We all make mistakes

PRACTICALS

- ➢ Own your mistakes. Completely let it go. Once you accept it, you can work on positive changes and embrace freedom

- ➢ Stop being captive to any resentments or grudges you have struggled with and start focusing on what is important now

- ➢ Focus on your morals and values now. Think about how things are different now compared to the past. You will get a better understanding of why you are hurting which gets you closer to the path of Self-Forgiveness

Be Kind to Yourself

It is always important to be kind to yourself. Self-Care is one of the most important key factors to allowing yourself to accept your reality. Focus on your truth and take care of yourself. Here are five ways to be kind:

- ➢ Treat yourself the way you would want others to treat you. We tend to treat ourselves much worse than we do others. Stop putting so much pressure on yourself

- ➢ Love yourself. Remind yourself you are unique and you are a great person that deserves to be loved by others, including yourself
- ➢ Give yourself a break. Allow yourself to make mistakes. Nobody is perfect. We all make mistakes while we learn and grow

- Build yourself up with confidence, and allow others to compliment you as well. Acknowledge your greatness. Focus on your progress, and realize how much you have grown as a person (Mentally/Physically/Spiritually)

- Never allow others to put you down. Once you accept how amazing you are, no one can hurt you or bring you down (walk away/ignore haters)

Positive Thoughts Daily

Positive Thinking is a mental attitude where you expect good and favorable results from any situation. One way I have accepted my new life is by my positive thinking. Once you rewire your brain to think positive daily, the negative situations will not stop you. Here are some examples of positive thinking:

- Focus on what makes you happy, what keeps you alive, and continue to fight. What inspires you in your day-to-day life? (Family/Friends/Purpose/Passion, etc.)

- Drink and eat as much healthy nutrients as possible. Research has shown that what you consume in your body can have huge influence on your emotional state of mind.
- Make sure you get at least 6-8 hours of sleep nightly. It has been proven that sleep deprivation causes extreme negative thinking (Anger/Depression/Irritability, etc.)

PRACTICALS

- Flip your negatives into positives. Take a negative situation and think about how you can flip it into a positive. One example of how you can flip your thought process is if something doesn't work out for you, it's often because the universe has something better in store. Remind yourself that either it's not the right time, or something better will happen

- Showing Positivity is a great way to receive positivity back. Be kind to others, show love and inspiration. Take the time to help strangers by doing small favors. This act will help put you in a better frame of mind (Groceries/Advise/Rides, etc.)

Focus

Focus is the third phase on the journey to Recovery. Now that you have a happier, healthier Mindset, and you have Accepted the truth about your life and circumstances around you, now you can focus on your mission. These next five topics will show you some of the best ways that I have taken myself from a basic "Veteran Mindset" to the "Veteran Mindset 2.0" by focusing on what needs to be done every day. We will talk about some techniques and lessons I have learned to gain my success.

Eliminate Pointless Distractions

When negative things are happening and it does not affect you personally, leave it alone. Staying out of other people's business is a huge plus. Stop stressing over other people's lives and situations. If it does not concern you. Stay out of it. Here is what to do instead:

- ➤ Focus on your own missions. Worrying and stressing over things you cannot change is pointless. Direct your focus on you and your task

- ➤ Break away. Isolate during your focus times. If you need to get work, schoolwork, or a job done, breaking away to quite places are a must. Loud noises, people, and music is pointless to be around when you need to concentrate on a task

- Studies have shown that small amounts of caffeine are ok. If lacking energy is a daily problem, using caffeine can help you focus better on your mission. Everybody is different. If caffeine is not an option for you, remember exercise, diet, and healthier drinks are also an option

- Stop overthinking everything. Most of the time when we struggle with certain mental conditions, it causes us to focus on other things that serve no purpose in our lives, as well as, the things that we cannot change no matter what we do. This is common in children and adults. "Day Dreaming", "Flash Backs", "Zoning Out", are examples, but, of course, all these depends on your own situation. Here are some examples of the most common mental health conditions that require medications and/or other resources (ADD/ADHD, PTSD, Depression, Bipolar, OCD, Anxiety)

There are several conditions that Veterans struggle with daily and It is up to you and your doctor to figure out what your struggles are and what works best for you. If you are serious about creating a better, happier mindset, then you have to get better at eliminating pointless distractions.

Removing Emotional Stress

Removing stress from your life is one of the key factors to getting to Recovery. Being stressed out is one of the six major causes of deaths in the US. Stress causes so many problems in our lives and most people do not even realize it. Stress causes things like Depression, Anxiety, Isolation, and one of the major reasons we are so distracted with negativity. In these next examples, I will show you some ways on how you can begin to learn to have a stress-free life using different techniques and information I have learned, as well as, showing you options that will help you develop a 2.0 Mindset:

- ➤ Stress comes in many forms. I call it Long-Term Stress and Short-Term Stress. LTS is something that you have stressed about for a long period of time or it's stress that comes with PTSD and other conditions. STS is a type of stress you suddenly get from bad situations. The difference between the two is that your stress level gets better as a situation gets better

- ➤ Studies also show that stress is a major reason we have so many Veteran suicides. It can wreak havoc on your Mind, Body, and Soul. Many Veterans, once they get out of service, start to stress out. (Life/Finances/VA/Relationships/Children, etc.) We may have to focus on these things but don't stress about what needs to be done. Just get it done without complaining

- ➤ Stress is something that we can get better at controlling with a lot of practice. (Practice makes perfect) Reading and learning about stress or taking certain medications can also have a positive effect that may help you focus during important tasks. Talk with your doctor about options

➢ Talk with inspiring and positive people who have learned how to cope and handle stress. Learning from those who have been through it is a great way to defeat stress. Inspiring talks, motivational audios, meditations, and Yoga are other great ideas I have used

➢ Stepping away from stressful situations is also key. Sometimes it is the environment we live in or it could be the things that stress us that we even enjoy, for example, social media, projects, side jobs, and relationships. Whatever it is, take some time away

Stay Alert, Stay Alive

As a Combat Veteran, I have heard this term so many times during my Army years. It has literally been molded in my brain. Focusing on what is going on around you is key to survival. This does not only apply on the battlefield, but real life, too. This is your life. Bunker down and focus on today's mission. These next examples we will cover are techniques and strategies on how and why it is important to stay focused on your mission. How does staying alert help you stay alive?

- Staying alert and recognize that your mind and body works like a machine. When there is a problem and something is not working correctly, it will let you know. Once you notice an issue going on with you, address it and focus on doing what it takes to get better. This is how you stay alive

- Remind yourself the reasons you want change. What are you tired of struggling with? Focus on your goals. Focus on the changes you want. (Success, Relationships, Personal Missions, Mindset, Weight, etc.) Whatever the goal, stick to it

- Do your best to focus on positivity daily. There are good days and bad days. Roll with the punches and always look for the good in people. Do not only focus on the bad things about people. We all have "bad days", so never judge a person by their own personal problems

- What does your "End Game" look like? Are you doing what it takes to not only get through each day, but planning for your end goal? Set yourself up with a 5-year and a 10-year plan. Focusing on today is key, but planning for your future is absolute

- Focusing on how far you have come is a great advantage to staying positive. Do not stress about how far you have left on the journey. Anything great takes time. Remember, this is your story and you are the one writing it. Everything you have been going through is just part of the plan. If you take your struggles and learn from them, you will make it. Anybody that is successful at business or in life with happiness and joy had to go through struggles and failures. Keep your head up and keep moving forward

Multitasking

Multitasking can be a tricky conversation when you ask people about it. The reason I say that is because many people that have busy lives tend to multitask more often than others. However, if you are someone that is struggling with your Mental Health and can't focus on one task, then obviously multitasking is not for you. These next examples we will cover is how multitasking can cause more harm than good:

- ➤ Multitasking has been shown to reduce your efficiency and performance because your brain can only focus on one thing at a time. If you need to focus on multiple tasks, work on each one separately at scheduled times so that each task is done successfully

- ➤ Studies have also shown that multitasking can lead to memory problems. Anyone with PTSD and ADHD and other conditions already understand how stressful memory loss can be. If you are serious about having a healthy mindset, stop with the multitasking. It's not helping you

- ➤ Multitasking can also lead to increased distractibility. Focusing on too many distractions at once has shown that a person loses the ability to distinguish between important and unimportant situations. This brings us back to "Staying Alert, Staying Alive." It's always important to focus on one task at a time

➢ One of the major things that I had to learn the hard way with trying to multitask is that it makes you less productive and less efficient. You might feel like you are getting a lot done at the time but chances are that you have to keep fixing mistakes. That is why, for example, this workbook gives you each step one at a time. You will not be able to focus on each step and understand it if you try to do them all at once. Take the time needed to understand what it is you are trying to learn

➢ Veterans that struggle with Mental Health and other conditions have been proven that keeping happy relationships are a huge challenge. Too many people try to do too much at once like focusing on all the negativities and not focusing on their relationships. Multitaskers have caused their partners to experience significantly reduced relationship happiness. A few examples are phones, computers, social media, etc.

Live in the Moment

You have heard me talk about living in the moment multiple times in this book. One reason is because living for today is so vital to changing your mindset to the 2.0 version. The next examples you will read will break down why it is

PRACTICALS

important, as well as, showing you some ways, I have been able to focus more on my "now." "Focus on today for a better tomorrow"

- ➢ Living in the moment simply means what it sounds like. Live for your "now." Focus on today's mission. Every day is a new day and a new mission you must work on

- ➢ Veterans that struggle from traumatic events tend to replay those events over and over in their mind. PTSD is the most common reason why Veterans struggle with their past and cannot live in the moment. However, once you reach a 2.0 mindset you will discover that anything is possible

- ➢ Living in the moment has many benefits, including helping you focus on your current goals. Focusing on your "now" means something different to each person. It all depends on what it is you need to work on at the moment. If you want to get better at things like marriage, career, school, projects, or mindset, you can do that now because you are more focused on your mission. You are now focusing on what needs to happen and living in the moment

- ➢ Be grateful and appreciative of everything you have in your life. Treat your small achievements like your big ones. Anything you have acquired from hard work, be proud of it. Once you show the Universe, and/or God, your gratitude, doors begin to open that you never thought possible. It starts with you being humble and grateful

- The act of gratitude has been scientifically linked to lowering your anxiety, stress, and depression. Hunt the good stuff every day by counting three blessings you are grateful for and sharing those blessings with someone, or even on social media. This spreads more positivity. Encourage others to engage in this practice

- The biggest lesson I learned is this: In order for me to become a better man, become great at what I do, and change my life, I knew I had to put in the work now. Too many times we put it off, saying, "I'll get to it tomorrow" and that is a huge mistake. Anybody that wants positive change in their lives must start immediately. Success waits for no one. If you want it, you go get it!

PRACTICALS

Self-Worth

Self-Worth is the 4th phase to Recovery. The key to get to Recovery is learning how to build your Self-Worth again. Some might say that it sounds simple enough, but it's not. As you probably already understand, Self-Worth does not always come easy. Just like anything else that you work with, practice is going to help you. Understand that your worth is based all on you. Nobody else determines your worth or how you feel about yourself. These next topics we will cover is why Self-Worth is important, how to obtain it, and what are some common ways it can destroy us by not having it. To get to the next level, you need to learn the causes and symptoms of struggling with no Self-Esteem.

Never Settle for Less

> ➢ "Settling for less" means that you don't know your Self-Worth and so you put yourself in the category of people that have no desires to win. You do not believe you're good enough and so you have the "take what you can get" attitude

> ➢ Be comfortable in your "own skin." Always love yourself. This will help you to not be affected by other's opinions. You know your worth

- ➢ A huge benefit of knowing your self-worth is that you no longer feel the need to belong to certain social groups and the feeling of having to "prove yourself" to others

- ➢ Removing people in your life that bring you no value. Surround yourself with greatness. Get away from those people that do not desire a positive successful future

- ➢ Studies show that one reason so many Veterans struggle with depression and suicide is because they "settle for less." If you believe that your life is worthless, then you are more likely to give up and settle for anything that you think makes you happy

Building Confidence

- ➢ Start building your confidence by believing in yourself, acknowledging your success, and your achievements. Take compliments and positive feedback

- ➢ Work on being more sociable. Connect with others around you. Be willing to connect with those that agree or disagree with your way of life. Be confident in who you are; others will see the confidence within you

- ➢ Build up your confidence by also reminding yourself daily that you are a good person. Write down positive good things that are in your life. Write down good things that you have done for others, not for ego purposes, but for confidence

➢ Exercise and eat healthier. Our appearance has a huge effect on our self-confidence. It's ok to want to "look good" for you. Dress to win, be bold, and be confident. This is your life

➢ Always do the right things. This is also another way to build up your confidence. You can lay your head down at night with ease knowing that you have done everything the right way and that you put 100% effort in your mission. Treat people the way that you want to be treated and be a positive good person that encourages others

Accepting Rejection

➢ The thing about rejection is that it usually involves something we really want. However, it is not always a bad thing. Here is the reason why I say that. Rejection shows us that you are not living inside your comfort zone. The more you live outside your comfort zone, you are more likely to be rejected, and that is ok. It shows that you are pushing yourself to your limits

➢ Rejection can also destroy a person's mindset and Self-Esteem, especially one that is already struggling with Self-Confidence. Nobody enjoys rejection but understand that everyone goes through it on the way to success. To be successful, you are going to experience some form of rejection

- ➢ Remember just because you have been turned down for a job, love interest, or a project, you should never declare yourself too incompetent. The right opportunities happen at the right time. Keep pushing forward!

- ➢ Always keep rejection in a proper perspective as far as your Mindset. One person's opinion or even a single incident does not define who you are as a person. Just because someone else thinks something about you, does not mean it is true. Remember, know your truth

- ➢ Use rejection as an opportunity to move forward with more wisdom. With each rejection, use it to grow stronger and become better. You must become mentally strong and know your Self-Worth in order to learn and grow when rejection comes

Truths About Trauma

- ➢ There are many ways to get a grip on your traumatic experience and build your Self-Esteem. First, it is important to understand that you are not alone in this fight. Find the Veterans in your community that have similar experiences. Listening to their stories is huge in understanding that you can get help and that you are not alone. Now is the time to start focusing on the things that make you happy and

PRACTICALS

work on getting the bad thoughts out of your mind. Use Meditations, Yoga, Focus Groups, Support Groups, Positive Talks, etc. These are great ways to help you gain more confidence and build your Self-Worth

➢ Many studies have shown that Traumatic Events have a huge impact on our Mindset and Self-Esteem. Some of the other symptoms are feelings of worthlessness and no longer belonging. Isolation is also a huge side effect because most of the time we do not have any Self-Worth, so people would rather be left alone and stay miserable. One way to break it down even deeper is that they would rather stay in their comfort zone or safe space

➢ There are many mental health conditions that Veterans struggle with, from Trauma, to Addiction, Depression, and Anxiety Disorders. There is the most common diagnosis of TBI (Traumatic Brain Injury) and PTSD (Post Traumatic Stress Disorder) that Veterans struggle with when coming out of a Combat Zone

➢ Understand that traumatic events can happen anywhere, any time. The truth is many Veterans that struggle with their Mental Health may not have suffered from traumatic experiences from Combat. Veterans that struggle with trauma are happening every day outside the Military. Car wrecks, OD, child trauma, physical assault, sexual assault, robbery, and death are some examples of traumatic events outside of combat. The reason I bring this up is because not everybody is a Combat Veteran and we all struggle with certain mental health issues for many different reasons

➢ Another way to help you cope with trauma and negative mental health is to give yourself a break. Too many times we are way too hard on ourselves. We have been trained to have a Military mentality and expect everything to be perfect and in order. Step back and take yourself back to accepting your reality. You are no longer Active Duty, so you don't have to live your life with the same Military Standards and Codes. It's ok to live by certain Codes like Loyalty, Honor, Respect, and so on. In the Army, we live by "7 Core Values" that keep us moving forward. Honestly in my opinion, we should continue to live by those 7 Core Values, even after our time in service. The one thing you need to understand is this: you do not have to be "perfect." You're allowed to make mistakes. Remind yourself daily that "It's Ok." You have been through so much and you deserve to relax and take care of yourself

Low Self-Esteem

➢ People with Low Self-esteem are easy to spot when you are associated with them. You can see it, hear it, and feel the low confidence and the negative attitude they have. Usually if you are struggling with any kind of self-confidence issue, you will not try new things or be sociable with others, and you most likely are an angry person and have a lot of anxiety. For many Veterans, struggling with Addiction plays a huge factor, as well. Of course, depending on the traumatic events you have suffered from, the symptoms can vary

- ➢ To understand low Self-Esteem is to understand the signs and symptoms. Even though we all struggle from different issues, we still have some common symptoms. Those people that suffer cannot handle criticism or praise. I have been guilty with both of these while I was struggling with my own Self-Esteem and Self-Worth issues. I constantly lived with the mindset that "I was never good enough." So, I never knew how to take someone giving me a complement. On the flip side, I struggled daily with the "can't do" attitude, and when I was told that something was not good enough or something needed more work on a project from my boss, spouse, friend or even a stranger, I would get angry and upset. The most common response is "I told you I couldn't do it" or "I knew I would fail" or "I quit" or "I am stupid." If you find yourself saying these words, there is no doubt you need to work on your Self-Worth

- ➢ Over time, low Self-Esteem will take a toll on a person. It makes people afraid to live life and try new things. Having such low Self-Esteem is just another reason why Veteran suicide is so high. The good news is all this can be managed. It takes hard work, dedication, and most of all, practice

- ➢ Many of our thoughts and feelings are locked in our subconscious mind. Writing about the way we feel and think in a journal will help with the negative ideas. Write about your daily journey. Talk about how you felt in certain situations. It is important to get it all out like you were talking to a friend. Express your truth

- ➢ Stay connected to yourself. Being mindful can help you build a connection with yourself and stop worrying about pleasing others before your own needs. Focusing on you is not selfish, it is needed. Building a 2.0 Mindset takes hard work and practice. You must uplift your Self-Esteem to know your Self-Worth. You are an amazing person and you can do anything you put your mind to.

PRACTICALS

Recovery

Welcome to the 5th and final phase of this workbook. Recovery is the last stage for building a 2.0 Mindset. It is important to understand that Recovery does not mean you are cured from any Mental Health condition you suffer from or any addictions. Recovery in this book simply means you are now living a life that you have only dreamed of. You understand you still have struggles, but now you see things so much clearer. You are now focused on your goals and your dreams of living a happy and successful life. You are no longer going to allow your Mental Health to define you as a person. Being in Recovery means that you have taken the proper steps to build a Mindset of positivity and happiness. In these next key topics, we will discuss the benefits of having a 2.0 Mindset, the benefits of being in Recovery, and some ways that will help you stay in your new Mindset and continue on the right path allowing you to stay on your mission.

Staying in Recovery

> ➤ Getting to Recovery is half the battle, but staying in recovery, is the real mission. It takes hard work and dedication to get to the Recovery phase and it takes just as much work to stay there

- Recovery does not mean you are cured. You have learned Coping Skills, Strategies, and Techniques to live a 2.0 Mindset with Mental Health conditions, or Addiction. Being in Recovery does not mean you will no longer struggle, but now you know how to deal with your issues and continue to live a happier life

- Keep taking care of yourself, especially on the days you don't feel like it. It's important to keep pushing yourself to the limits. Remember to take the breaks needed when you hit roadblocks and always refocus on your mission. Adjust fire if needed

- Pay close attention to your Mind, Body, and Soul. Each one of these plays a vital role to staying in recovery. Continue to work on your positive thought process, exercise daily to keep your body in shape and healthy, and work on Meditations, Prayer, and Affirmations every morning to keep your spirit fresh, positive, and full of life

- Remind yourself of the reasons you wanted to grow mentally and emotionally in the first place. Never lose sight of your goals. A lot of times after we have grown to the next level in our lives, things like roadblocks and unexpected issues may occur and begin to stress you out. Just remember how far you have come and why you are making progress.

PRACTICALS

Victim Mentality

➢ Too many Veterans, and people in general, fail because they put themselves in the "Victim Mentality" Mindset. Sometimes bad things happen to us, either in Combat, or outside the Military. Maybe you are a victim, however, it is important to be strong, face your circumstances, and don't play the "blame game" regardless of the situation. If your goal is to stay in the 2.0 Mindset, you must accept it and move forward

➢ Take ownership and responsibility of your wants, needs, and actions. You are the only one responsible for your own thoughts. When you hear yourself going into the "blame game", try telling yourself out loud, "Stop" or "No", and turn your attention away from your blaming thoughts

➢ At certain times during your healing process, getting to Recovery you may want to blame people, the Military, or even the whole world for your problems. Remember to read back to the chapter on "Acceptance" to remind yourself that there is nothing you can do to change your trauma or situation that hurt you, but you can accept it and "Focus" on what you can do to improve your situations, even if it feels impossible

➢ There is nothing good about living a victim mentality. However, you can change your outcome and your thoughts by following this workbook combined with the desire to change. A life lived with gratitude and kindness is much better than living a life full of resentment and bitterness. Empowerment and self-command are available to everyone, but it takes a winning attitude and new behaviors

- ➢ Playing the victim role means you are deciding to hold onto bitterness and anger, and you are living with the thought that you have been mistreated or wronged by the Universe or God for things you cannot control. Remember, you got to Recovery by focusing on the positive things in your life, not the negativity. I had to learn much of this the hard way, I said things like, "Why me?", "Why now?", "Why does God hate me?", "Why do bad things keep happening to me?", until I figured out that I control how I feel. I continued to live like a victim. Remember, you can't control the bad shit from happening, but you can control how you react to it

Living with Gratitude

- ➢ Why does having gratitude matter when staying in Recovery? Gratitude is strongly and consistently associated with greater happiness, being thankful for the things and positive people in your life. It makes you appreciate what you have rather than what you don't have. Gratitude is the most powerful source of inspiration that will help you stay focused in a 2.0 Mindset

- ➢ Having Gratitude will not only help you stay in a positive mindset and stay happier, but it will also help you through certain mental health challenges

PRACTICALS

Anxiety, Depression, and PTSD are some examples that gratitude will help with. Gratitude reduces the stress hormones and managing the autonomic nervous system functions. It will greatly reduce many of the symptoms that are associated with Anxiety, Depression, and PTSD. Focusing on the good things in life will help you stay in the "Recovery Mindset"

➢ Studies have shown many benefits from having Gratitude. Some of those benefits from having Gratitude seems to open many more doors to success and relationships. It has shown to help you sleep better at night, as well as, feeling psychologically and physically healthier. You can influence more people around you to be better by how you present yourself and showing your positive attitude

➢ Having Gratitude for everything in your life is not always an easy task. The fact is, you have been through so much in your life that sometimes you just can't help but to expect the worse out of people and out of life, in general. Most of us that have suffered with mental health that came from trauma or other things just have a hard time seeing the good in things. Focus on one good thing at a time. Write down in your daily journal what you are thankful every day and start from there

➢ If you are looking to keep a Veteran Mindset 2.0, you must keep in mind that being grateful for your life and the things in your life is key. Understand that if you cannot seem to keep any gratitude for anything, you need to go back in this workbook and start over. First step should be that you're grateful for the opportunity to be able to change your life and your mindset. Start small and work your way up to bigger things. We should always have a certain amount of Gratitude towards our children, family, and good friends. I am grateful that I have found my purpose and passion which is to write this book to help millions of people achieve a Veteran Mindset 2.0. Keep working at it daily. You got this!

2.0 Environment

- There are many ways to stay in the Recovery Mindset. One of the biggest lessons I have learned from being a child and into adult hood is that it is all about your environment. We are who we surround ourselves with. I have said it many times in this workbook and I will say it again. Removing "Toxic" people from your life is a must. The fact is that if you want to continue to stay at a 2.0 Mindset, you need 2.0 friends

- Focus on surrounding yourself with winners. Put yourself in the kind of places that successful people hangout. Try giving more value and take less from others. Show other people that you are a Leader and that you are going to be successful. Use your leadership skills from the Military and apply it in the world. Most people trust Veterans, so use that once you get to know someone new

PRACTICALS

- It is not only important to find the right people, but it is also important to find like-minded people. These people will understand the path you are trying to go to. Find the same people with the same drive to better themselves. They will know what it takes to reach your goals and it will help you stay confident and positive

- Keeping your mindset positive is the key factor to being successful with achieving your goals. One way is to hang out with positive influencers. It will become so much easier to stay focused on your end game. You will feel so much better about yourself. You will feel more energized and motivated to get the important things done

- Keeping a 2.0 Mindset is going to be a huge challenge. Be proud of yourself for coming this far. Surround yourself with people that want to see you succeed and become the person you hope to be. Make sure you are showing the same support to those same people that are supporting you. Become the kind of person that you want to be around. Soon you will find those same type of people reaching out to you. Keep your positive attitude and watch your life continue to grow. I am so proud of you!

Practice

- One thing is for sure that we all know the saying, "Practice Makes Perfect." This goes for anything you do in life. This also includes you staying at a 2.0

Mindset. You must keep doing what it takes over and over to gain perfection

- ➢ Practicing everything that you have learned in this workbook will be your reward. Practicing the skills and techniques that you have learned will cause those neural pathways to work better in unison. The mission here is to form muscle memory

- ➢ Learning how to live a happier and healthier lifestyle takes practice just like learning how to play sports or cooking. Learning any new skills can be hard at the beginning, but the more you do it, the easier it becomes. Starting from a Basic Mindset to a 2.0 Mindset takes hard work and practice. Keep learning and studying and you will become a master of your 2.0 Mindset

- ➢ There are many techniques and strategies in this workbook to help you achieve the Veteran Mindset 2.0. The most import factor is to have the desire to want change. You also need to be willing to put in the work and keep an open mind. Never forget why you started this mission. Focus on what is important to you and you will achieve anything you want. Successful people that have struggled in the past with Addiction, Mental Health, or even suicidal thoughts, will tell you to practice every day and you will reach your goals

- ➢ Practice, Practice, Practice! Nobody ever becomes a pro by not practicing. I have stressed this because I need you to understand what it means to practice. Once you have made it to a life of Recovery, you are

PRACTICALS

going to live a brand-new life. You will finally start to believe in yourself and know your Self-Worth. You will be so proud of yourself that you will start to look and feel different about yourself. Keep moving forward in your journey and you will become a positive influencer for friends and family members who have seen you grow. Do not let up on your mission, and one day, you just might save a fellow Veteran's life

QUESTIONS

QUESTIONS

In this section of the book, you can check where your own mindset is at. I have created 11 questions you can answer that are based on each lesson that you have learned. This is simply a way for you to see how much you need to grow and use it as a study guide. There are no right or wrong answers, but I would encourage you to use the practicals section to help you.

Mindset:

Answer the questions to the best of your ability with three answers each. (Refer back to practice)

1. Why is having the right Mindset important to get to recovery?

   ➢

   ➢

   ➢

2. What does a Veteran Mindset 2.0 mean to you?

   ➢

   ➢

   ➢

3. What is a Growth Mindset?

   ➢

   ➢

➤

4. Give three examples of Positive Talks

➤
➤

➤

5. Name 5 ways you can create a Healthy Mindset

➤

➤

➤

➤

➤

6. What are 3 ways to keep yourself inspired and motivated?

➤

➤

➤

7. Why is having a positive support system important?

➤

➤

➤

QUESTIONS

8. Explain what "Turning your Mess into your Message" means?

   ➢

   ➢

   ➢

9. Give 3 daily goals you can use to grow your Mindset

   ➢

   ➢

   ➢

10. What are 3 challenging obstacles in your life that you can turn into opportunities?

    ➢

    ➢

    ➢

Millions of Veterans struggle every day with Mental Health, Addiction, and Suicidal Thoughts. We lose on average 22 Veterans every day to suicide.

Bonus Question:
11. In your own words, explain how upgrading your Mindset to the 2.0 Version is going to or has improved your quality of life?

-
-
-

Acceptance:
Answer the questions to the best of your ability with 3 answers each.
(Refer back to the practice)

1. What does Acceptance mean?

   -
   -
   -

2. Why is accepting your current situation important?

   -
   -
   -

QUESTIONS

3. Give 3 reasons why "letting go of the past" is so important

   ➢

   ➢

   ➢

4. What are 3 things you can do to help you accept your Mental Health conditions?

   ➢

   ➢

   ➢

5. What are 3 ways your life will improve once you learn to accept your current circumstances?

   ➢

   ➢

   ➢

6. When you accept a person(s) opinion, does that mean you have to approve of it as well? Explain with 3 answers. Yes or No

   ➢

   ➢

   ➢

7. Give 3 examples of any situations that you will need to accept in order to grow

   ➤

   ➤

   ➤

8. Forgiveness plays a huge role in Acceptance. Name 3 reasons why forgiveness is important

   ➤

   ➤

   ➤

9. In your own words, explain 3 things that you feel friends and family members don't understand about you

   ➤

   ➤

   ➤

10. What are 3 things that you have had to accept about yourself to get to Recovery?

    ➤

    ➤

    ➤

QUESTIONS

Bonus Question:
11. Name your 3 best Strengths and your 3 worse Weaknesses

Strengths

➢

➢

➢

Weakness

➢

➢

➢

Focus:
Answer the questions to the best of your ability with three answers each
(Refer back to the practice)

1. What is Focus?

➢

➢

➢

2. Why is Focus important for Recovery?

➢

➢

➢

3. What are 3 difficulties you struggle with when trying to focus?

➢

➢

➢

4. What are 3 ways to help you focus better on your mission?

➢

➢

➢

5. What are 3 benefits from learning to focus?

➢

➢

➢

QUESTIONS

6. Give 3 examples of some weekly goals you are going to focus on

   -
   -
   -

7. Write down 5 distractions that you struggle with daily that keeps you from focusing

   -
   -
   -
   -
   -

8. Write down 5 ways that will help you defeat those distractions

   -
   -
   -
   -
   -

Stress affects us all. One major thing about stress is that it can keep you from focusing on your goals.

9. What are 3 ways you can eliminate your stress?

➢

➢

➢

10. What are 3 things you can do to help you focus?

➢

➢

➢

Affirmations are key to a healthy mindset. They also help you stay focused on your mission.

Bonus Question:
11. What are 3 Affirmations that help you daily with focus?

➢

➢

➢

QUESTIONS

Self-Worth:

Answer the questions to the best of your ability with three answers
(Refer back to practice)

1. What is Self-Worth?

    ➢

    ➢

    ➢

2. Why is having Self-Worth important to Recovery?

    ➢

    ➢

    ➢

3. What are 3 ways to help build your Self-Worth?

    ➢

    ➢

    ➢

4. Explain what "Love yourself the same way you love others" means

    ➢

    ➢

-

Never settle for less. You deserve the world.

5. Write down 3 reasons why you believe your answer to Question 4

-
-
-

6. Write down 5 reasons why you believe you are a good person

-
-
-
-
-

7. Why is it important to be kind and helpful to others?

-
-
-

QUESTIONS

8. What are 3 examples of any accomplishments you are proud of?

 ➢

 ➢

 ➢

9. Why is it important to have fun and be around positive people?

 ➢

 ➢

 ➢

10. Write down 5 positive things that are in your life

 ➢

 ➢

 ➢

 ➢

 ➢

Removing "Toxic" people from your life is key to success and happiness. Toxic people will destroy your Mindset and Self-Esteem.

Bonus Question:

11. Explain in your own words why removing "Toxic" people from your environment is important?

>
>
>

Recovery:

Answer all the questions to the best of your ability with three answers
(Refer back to practice)

1. What does Mental Health Recovery mean?

>
>
>

2. Why is Recovering from a negative Mental Health important?

>
>
>

QUESTIONS

3. Explain why it is important to push yourself to the limits while in Recovery

   ➢

   ➢

   ➢

4. List 3 reasons it is important to grow Mentally and Emotionally

   ➢

   ➢

   ➢

5. What are the 3 major areas you need to focus on while you are in recovery?

   ➢

   ➢

   ➢

6. Why is it important to keep positive people around you?

   ➢

   ➢

   ➢

7. Why is having a healthy Mindset important?

    ➢

    ➢

    ➢

8. As a Veteran, you have learned that "Charlie Mike" (Continue the Mission) is vital in any situation. Explain Why?

    ➢

    ➢

    ➢

9. What are 3 components of Recovery?

    ➢

    ➢

    ➢

10. Why is it important to learn about your own Mental Health diagnosis?

    ➢

    ➢

    ➢

Recovering from Mental Health is not an easy mission. You should be proud of yourself for getting this far. There are 5

QUESTIONS

major areas of your life you need to focus on to stay in Recovery.

Bonus Question:
11. What are the 5 key areas of your life you need to focus on to stay in Recovery?

- ➤
- ➤
- ➤
- ➤
- ➤

Veteran Mindset 2.0 Affirmations Guidelines

Here are some examples of my favorite Affirmations that I use to get to a 2.0 Mindset and get my day started. Remember, creating a positive and healthy mindset takes practice. Repeating these affirmations will help you with a Growth Mindset and Personal Development. Here are five important things for you to remember before you start using your affirmations daily:

- ➢ Every morning when you wake up or during your meditation times pick at least 5 affirmations and repeat them as many times as you need to.

- ➢ You can repeat them anytime that you like. But I found using affirmations every morning or every night is best when you can focus.

- ➢ Focus on the affirmations that you need the most to help you grow in your life.

- ➢ It is important not to overwhelm yourself with too many affirmations at once. These are made to help build your confidence and your own self-worth.

VETERAN MINDSET 2.0 AFFIRMATIONS GUIDELINES

> ➢ **Repeating your affirmations in a quiet place. Having zero distractions during meditation will work best for you.**

Affirmations
(1-32)

> ➢ I am confident and exhilarated knowing my actions today will create momentum tomorrow and the next day.

> ➢ I feel unstoppable.

> ➢ I am free of the fear of rejection. Rejection is a necessary thing to achieve success.

> ➢ I am enough, I am smart, helpful and worthy Knowing I am good enough makes me feel comfortable, confident and exhilarated.

> ➢ I do not fear mistakes or failure. Mistakes and failure are necessary to achieve success.

> ➢ I feel happy and strong-minded knowing that I am free from judging others.

> ➢ I will not focus on what others are thinking and saying about me in a negative way.

> ➢ I enjoy calling my prospects and customers on the phone. Each call is a new opportunity to build a relationship and help somebody.

> ➢ I know that right now, somewhere, someone's life is getting better and more prosperous because of my products and services.

- I feel confident and excited about moving on to new opportunities every day.

- My positive affirmations, my goal-setting and my constant actions make me an incredibly successful person.

- I am an incredibly positive and a strong-minded person

- I love exercising and consuming healthy foods.

- I attract success and success is attracted to me

- Success comes to me easily. I love waking up each day knowing that success is guaranteed for me.

- I am a self-starter and a motivator

- I am a motivated and energetic person and I feel good every day.

- I am proud of myself and my success.

- I have a powerful body, powerful mind, and powerful Soul.

- I am smart and deserving of the world's greatest levels of success.

- I always speak my words with confidence and conviction.

VETERAN MINDSET 2.0 AFFIRMATIONS GUIDELINES

- My words are powerful and they bring knowledge, confidence and truth to other people.

- I am a happy and grateful person

- Nobody can stop me from being the best.

- I excel at everything I do and I always feel like a winner.

- I know I am deserving of huge financial wealth and respect.

- I have inner strength, passion, and the confidence to win at whatever I choose to do.

- I am optimistic and filled with enthusiasm.

- I complete all my projects and my work every day on time.

- I am grateful, smart, powerful, and courageous

- I always give more than what I get back. I choose to be a good person.

Made in the USA
Coppell, TX
04 May 2021